What people are saying about Barbara Hemphill and *Taming the Paper Tiger at Work*

"A valuable tool for anyone who works in an office, whether a corner suite or a corner of the kitchen. Clear, practical and in touch with today's work environment."

THOMAS C. NELSON, PHD
Chief Operating Officer, AARP

"I find your books to be among the most truly helpful guides for modern living ever written and will continue to be a disciple of your work. Please keep it coming—your clutter-free, organized wanna-be's are waiting!"

DIANE E. HORVATH
Director of Special Projects, Virginia Information Providers Network

"Following Barbara Hemphill's advice, we eliminated enough paper to fill an entire office in our building. We have improved our efficiency with Barbara's help, which allows us to be more productive in carrying out our mission."

KEITH L. FISHBURNE
President, Special Olympics North Carolina, Inc.

"Barbara's easy-to-execute strategies and practical steps bring quick and easy-to-understand organization to even the most chaotic of office environments."

AL PETERSON
News/Talk/Sports Editor, Radio and Records, Los Angeles, Cal.

"Your system helped me the day I received your book and software in the mail. I've implemented my own little version of your filing system, and it has made a world of difference."

PAUL LEMBERG
Futurist, Strategist and Author, *How to Predict the Future of Just About Anything*

"Entrepreneurs everywhere will find *Taming the Paper Tiger at Work* an incredibly effective tool for dealing with all the stuff and messes a business creates, freeing them up to focus on achieving their goals."

DAN SULLIVAN
Founder, The Strategic Coach

"Taming the Paper Tiger at Work is a must-read for anyone who agonizes over what to keep, where to keep it and how to find it. It provides practical strategies on organizing any office to reduce stress and become more productive."

DANIEL BURRUS
Author, *Technotrends*

"Being 'organized,' especially when it came to the avalanche of paper that flows in and out of my office, was always an area of mega-stress. I needed a filing system for all of my messages, but also for the scattered pieces of paper containing spiritual insights that I hadn't fully developed into a completed message. Those are just two of a long list of solutions Paper Tiger has brought to me."

LEE DAVIS
Church Pastor

"Our organization has grown by 400% in the past year. Since paperwork is one of my greatest challenges, Paper Tiger manages the mounds of paper that have tied me down so that I am free to run my business more efficiently and effectively. I am grateful for this time-saving program and cannot even imagine how I functioned without it. It's as though I hired another person to work in my office."

JANELLE HAIL
Founder and President, The National Breast Cancer Foundation

"Barbara spent a morning in my store helping me to organize my office. I like going into my office now. Thanks to Barbara Hemphill, I'm in charge and the paper tiger is in the cage . (Well, actually it's in its file.)"

ELAINE PETROCELLI
President, Book Passage, Corte Madera, Cal.

"I use the 'six-foot rule' with Paper Tiger—I tell everyone who comes within six feet of me about it!"

JONATHAN WARD
Corporate Coach and Consultant

"Barbara Hemphill's advice, combined with my use of The Paper Tiger, has had a greater impact on my business than any investment I've made over the past six years. Thanks to her, I've learned more than how to be clutter-free. I've discovered how to be truly productive, which has enabled me to do more in less time, reduce stress, and provide superior customer service."

MARILYNN MOBLEY
Acorn Consulting Group, Inc.

"Barbara helped me discover how best to organize files, books, articles, etc., in a way that suits the specific needs of my office. Now that she has set up the system, we can find everything regardless of who originally filed it! We have saved hours collectively, because we are not wasting time looking for things. Our stress level has lowered since the piles of paper disappeared. Whether your business consists of one person or 1,000, if you are willing to release the old filing rules that do not work, Barbara Hemphill and Paper Tiger can help you create a system that works and is sustainable over time."

LENORA BILLINGS-HARRIS, CSP
President, Excel Development Systems, Inc.

Taming *the* Paper Tiger *at* Work

KIPLINGER'S BUSINESS MANAGEMENT LIBRARY
Business 2010
Cash Rules
Customer Once, Client Forever
Fast-Track Business Growth
Hunting Heads
Parting Company
Practical Tech for Your Business
Raising Capital
You Can't Fire Me, I'm Your Father

OTHER KIPLINGER BOOKS
But Which Mutual Funds?
Buying & Selling a Home
The Consumer's Guide to the Experts
Dollars & Sense for Kids
Financing College
Home•ology
Kiplinger's Practical Guide to Investing
Kiplinger's Practical Guide to Your Money
Know Your Legal Rights
Making Money in Real Estate
Next Step: The Real World
Retire & Thrive
Retire Worry-Free
Switching Careers
Taming the Paper Tiger at Home

Kiplinger offers excerpts and tables of contents for
all of our books on our Web site (www.kiplinger.com).

For information about volume discounts contact:

Cindy Greene
Kiplinger Books & Tapes
1729 H Street, N.W.
Washington, DC 20006
e-mail: cgreene@kiplinger.com
202-887-6431
cgreene@kiplinger.com

Taming *the* Paper Tiger *at* Work

BARBARA HEMPHILL

KIPLINGER BOOKS
Washington, DC

Published by
The Kiplinger Washington Editors, Inc.
1729 H Street, N.W.
Washington, D.C. 20006

Library of Congress Cataloging-in-Publication Data

Hemphill, Barbara.
    Taming the paper tiger at work / Barbara Hemphill.--3rd ed.
        p. cm.
    At head of title: Kiplinger's.
    Includes index.
    ISBN 0-938721-98-4(pbk.)
        1. Paperwork (Office practice)--Management. 2. Filing systems. 3. Time management.
    I. Title: Kiplinger's taming the paper tiger at work. II. Title.

HF5547.15 .H449 2002
651.5--dc21

2002075419

Clutter Is Postponed Decisions, Taming the Paper Tiger, The Art of Wastebasketry, The FAT System, and The Productivity Quickstart are registered trademarks of Barbara Hemphill. *The To Do Book* is copyright 1983 by Barbara Hemphill.

This publication is intended to provide guidance in regard to the subject matter covered. It is sold with the understanding that the author and publisher are not herein engaged in rendering legal, accounting, tax or other professional services. If such services are required, professional assistance should be sought.

Third edition. Printed in the United States of America.

9 8 7 6 5 4 3 2 1

Dedication

With much love and appreciation to my husband—and "resident archivist"—Alfred T. Taylor, Jr.

Acknowledgments

Frequently a consulting company is named "...& Associates" to imply that the company is larger than it may actually be. The reality is that any successful company needs "associates." I am no exception. I am continually blessed by people without whom I would not be able to do what I do. They include my family, who has always been supportive even when my efforts seemed ridiculous; my friends from around the world who provide encouragement and expertise when I need it most; my business colleagues, especially those from NAPO and NSA; and the people who so graciously supply the services I need, from designing my promotional materials to fixing my hair. And, of course, there are my clients—without whom there would be no Hemphill Productivity Institute.

I am very grateful to the many people who provided invaluable assistance in the continuing update of this book, especially D.J. Watson, my virtual assistant extraordinare, and her associate, Leigh Terjillo, and my office manager, Brooke Ballantyne.

A book is not a book until you have a publisher, and I am proud to be associated with Kiplinger Books and the people who worked tirelessly to make this book become a reality. My heartfelt thanks to: David Harrison, Director of Kiplinger Books, who has supported my passion for *Taming the Paper Tiger* from the first edition; Pat Mertz Esswein, who creatively edited this edition of the book; Cindy Greene, who provided editorial and marketing assistance; Heather Waugh, who designed the cover and interior of the book; Allison Leopold, who proofread the final pages of the book; and Jane Rea and Cathy Dettmar, of Editorial Experts, Inc., who provided the indexing.

I thank you all.

Barbara Hemphill

Contents

Introduction

Nearly a decade ago, we at the Kiplinger organization came across a wizard with an uncanny ability to teach people how to reduce the clutter of paper in their personal lives, thereby increasing their productivity and peace of mind.

This wizard is Barbara Hemphill, and we are proud to have published her highly acclaimed first book, *Taming the Paper Tiger at Home*, which has shown tens of thousands of Americans how to organize their information at home—everything from bills and legal documents to family photographs and memorabilia.

In her consulting practice, Ms. Hemphill also teaches businesspeople how to get a grip on their avalanche of paper, which continues unabated and in many cases has worsened since the advent of today's electronic tools. Her clear, easy-to-follow advice on organizing office information is available to all of us in this revised and updated edition of her second book, *Taming the Paper Tiger at Work*.

I know that our company needs help in this area, and I bet yours does, too. *The Kiplinger Letters*, which we've published for almost eight decades, are legendary for their crisp, clear and uncluttered writing. So you might assume that our desks and offices are a similar model of spare efficiency.

Well, that's not entirely the case. Like most people, we sometimes have trouble finding just the right documents, whether on paper or in a computer file. We hold onto things longer than we need to, and we sometimes feel overwhelmed by paper.

Computers and e-mail have helped a little, reducing the number of memos to photocopy and circulate and eliminating the little pink telephone-message slips. But it is still overly tempting to hit the "print" button and make a paper version of every electronic file, whether e-mail or pages from a useful Web site, creating a filing challenge in the process.

Barbara Hemphill offers some simple and very practical ideas for dealing with every aspect of information clutter and staying organized at work—for individual employees and for organizations as a whole. Her ideas for a company-wide File Clean-Out Day can be implemented by leaders at the top, who, she suggests, should set the example; by managers of individual departments; and by support staff, who may be charged with the task of keeping everyone and everything organized. She points out that the search for misplaced information consumes an inordinate amount of busy executives' time and results in significant losses in productivity.

My grandfather, W.M. Kiplinger, believed that busy people of the 1920s were overwhelmed with too much information to read and digest, and his pioneering work in newsletter journalism was a response to this concern. As quaint as the '20s concern might seem to us today, information overload was a problem back then. It's just a vastly bigger problem today.

Becoming better organized, at home and at the office, is a big job that, fortunately, can be divided into many small pieces and steps. *Taming the Paper Tiger at Work* will get you started and keep you on track. And it will pay you rich dividends for years to come, in improved business performance and personal satisfaction.

Knight Kiplinger

Knight Kiplinger
Editor in Chief, *The Kiplinger Letter* and *Kiplinger's Personal Finance Magazine*

Getting Centered

CHAPTER 1

Organize Your Thoughts

Do you recognize this scene? You sit down one morning determined to find your desk under that pile of papers. You pick up the first piece of paper and think of a number of reasons why you can't deal with it today. You pick up another piece, "Noooo, I don't think so…"

You remember that you haven't checked your voice-mail messages. You do so, taking notes as you go. The other phone line rings. You take more notes. You switch your attention to your e-mail messages. More notes. Before you know it, the stack of papers on the left side of your desk has crept to the right side, you've got a pile of note papers sitting in front of you, and today's e-mail messages are loitering in your electronic in-box, but they're no longer flagged as new or incoming.

Glancing at the clock, you realize you've got a meeting, but don't have a clue where the agenda is, or what room you're supposed to go to. *Yikes.* Your morning's off to a tough start—there's just too much of everything!

We're all bombarded with information. Even though we're solidly in the Computer Age, the promise of a paperless office has fallen flat. In fact, statistics show that the opposite has happened: There's more paper than ever. (So why can't you ever find something to write on?)

Paper truly is everywhere in our offices. Every event in your work life, from finding a job to retiring, produces paper. Instead of freeing us from paper's clutches, modern office equipment—super-fast copiers and computer printers—has become a kind of enabler, allowing many

You know the Paper Tiger has got *you* by the tail when your office is overflowing, you spend hours looking for information, and sometimes can't find it at all.

of us to turn our office into our own quick-print outlet. Office junk mail—a deluge of unwanted solicitations for supplies, seminars, professional publications, and so on—is a perennial problem. But now we add to it when we tap into various Web sites of interest or our e-mail accounts and print out reams of information and correspondence. Sure, some of this information is directed specifically to us, and much of it is not; some is related to work, and much of it is not. No matter what the situation, we might want the information someday. But until someday comes, all that stuff sits in heaps on our desks, around our workstations and in our files.

Certainly few people would want to return to doing manually what we can now do electronically, but we're faced with many new organizing challenges. It's tough enough to decide where to file a piece of paper, but now we must cope with computer files, directories, subdirectories, disks and drives. The challenge of organization is further complicated with the additions of voice mail, e-mail, cell phones and pagers.

What you're experiencing is the roar of the paper tiger. Perhaps it's only toying with you, but you know it's got *you* by the tail when your office is overflowing, you spend hours looking for information, and sometimes can't find it at all. Take a quick inventory. Do you:

- **Postpone returning phone calls** because you can't find the information you need to have an intelligent discussion now?
- **Forget** to return phone calls?
- **Have files jammed** with papers you haven't used in months—or even years?
- **Waste time** scrolling through your computer's directories looking for an important document?
- **Go to meetings unprepared,** lacking information that you need to make the strongest possible presentation or to get the information you need from others?
- **Meet someplace other than your office**—say, a conference room or restaurant—because you're embarrassed about how your office looks?
- **End up doing work** you could have delegated if you hadn't waited until it was too late to ask for help?

- **Blame other people** for your disorganization?
- **Drag work home** every night?

The tiger sleeps—and you have a temporary respite—when you ignore the papers, publications, messages, notes and stacks of unidentified floppies. But in the back of your mind is the fear that the tiger will awaken at any moment and rampage through your life.

You wake the tiger when you dig through piles—paper and electronic—and face disappointments, obligations, uncertainty, indecision, and the reality that you can't do all the things you want to do—or that you think you ought to do.

So now what? You're going to confront that tiger, that's what! By following the guidelines in this book, you'll tame the tiger and regain control of your work life.

What Organization Is— and Isn't

Let's face it—organization can be an extremely emotional issue. Some people resist organization because it will cramp their style—forcing them to become a neatnik, sacrifice creativity or conform to someone else's standard. Others believe that time is money and that spending time to get organized is unproductive and not cost-effective. For some, all those piles are a security blanket: "If I keep a copy of everything, I will avoid disaster." Even thinking about admitting to the need for getting organized can make people experience feelings that are often symptomatic of a misunderstanding about organization. Those feelings include:

- **Fear** (I might have to throw it out.)
- **Defiance** (I won't throw it out!)
- **Anger** (Why should I throw it out?)
- **Guilt** (Why didn't I throw it out?)
- **Shame** (I should have thrown it out!)

So, what is organization? Let me begin by saying what it is not.

> **Stress doesn't come from clutter—it comes from not knowing what to do with the clutter.**

ORGANIZING IS NOT A MORAL ISSUE, no matter what your mother may have told you. In fact, organizing in and of itself has no value. Its only value is that it helps you accomplish something important to you or your employer. The task itself is boring, but unless you do it, getting what you want—when you want it—becomes very difficult. Tom Landry, the former Dallas Cowboys football coach, once said, "My job is to make the guys do what they don't want to do, so they can be who they've always wanted to be." My role as an organizing consultant is very similar.

ORGANIZATION IS NOT NECESSARILY NEATNESS. Remember that old adage, "A place for everything and everything in its place"? Well, that statement is only half right: A place for everything is essential, but everything in its place depends on the person and situation. Stress doesn't come from clutter—it comes from not knowing what to *do* with the clutter. When I'm working, my desk is far from neat, but it takes only a few minutes to get it back in shape when there's a place for everything.

ORGANIZATION IS NOT A FINAL DESTINATION. In the normal course of events, and particularly during crises, things will get disorganized, or may simply have to change. Say that you organize your supply cabinet, and six weeks later it looks like a disaster again. That doesn't mean it is one—you just didn't have time to put things away in the right place. But if you organized the supplies effectively the first time, with clearly labeled containers, it'll be simple to get things back in the right order. Also, keep in mind that new responsibilities, work relationships, technologies or workspaces may force you to revise a system that used to work just fine.

ORGANIZATION DOES NOT ALWAYS EQUAL EFFICIENCY, BUT IT ALMOST ALWAYS EQUALS EFFECTIVENESS. Efficiency refers to the quickest way of accomplishing the mechanics of a task. But it can be a dangerous trap to spend time being efficient about things that don't matter. Instead, you must establish priorities by asking yourself these questions:

- **What needs doing?**
- **What needs doing first, second, last?**
- **Should I be doing this at all?**

Organization isn't a single way of doing things. One of my biggest professional frustrations is that an organizing consultant intimidates people. I often hear, "Ms. Green will meet you in the conference room," and discover that Ms. Green didn't want me to see her office! Or, after meeting me, someone says, "You would die if you saw my desk!" Prospective clients often fear that I'll pass judgment, or deem what they have done is wrong or bad.

Nothing could be further from the truth. There is no right or wrong in this—there's only what works for you. What you admire about your colleague's organization may not work for you, and that's okay.

Here are three of my basic organizing principles:

- **What you do doesn't matter,** as long as you do it consistently—or until you discover a better way. That concept allows for individual styles. For example, a friend of mine constantly makes lists, but she insists on using a variety of colors and sizes of notepads.
- **Does it work,** and do you like it?
- **Does it work for everyone?** This question is appropriate if your style or choice of organizing strategy affects other people.

> There is no right or wrong in getting organized—there's only what works for you.

Clutter Is Postponed Decisions

So many of us feel we should get organized, once and for all. But we don't. Why? Let's look at each of four main reasons I've encountered in my work:

- **We don't have time.**
- **We don't know how.**
- **We want to do it perfectly.**
- **We just don't want to do it.**

FROM MY FILES: START SOONER

Years ago after speaking at a press association meeting about how to improve organization skills, one very successful radio broadcaster came up to me and said, "You know, I've managed to accomplish a lot of things in my life, but it sure would have been easier if I had learned twenty years ago what you are teaching now." Her disorganization cost her time and energy and undoubtedly lost her opportunities.

I Don't Have the Time

Lack of time is a huge factor over which we don't always have control.

Not long ago, all executives, and most managers had a personal secretary whose time was dedicated to keeping the boss organized—files kept, messages delivered, correspondence filed or sent, schedule maintained, even gifts purchased and delivered. Thanks in part to corporate downsizing and business technology, most people no longer have such help. The remaining support staff members, each of whom reported to one or two people, now report to a dozen, and the managers who do survive downsizing now often do the work of two or more people.

Despite the demands of work and the advent of multitasking, we're still faced with a dilemma: Are you disorganized because you don't have time, or are you short on time because you're disorganized?

People often say, "Someday I'll get organized." But often that day never comes until a crisis hits. Your best bet is to spend time organizing to avoid, or at least minimize, the crises. Organization won't prevent a crisis but you'll have a better chance of coping if and when it occurs.

You don't need to spend huge amounts of time learning new things—often we can be more successful by just giving our routine a new twist. For example, if you find papers in your in-box that need to be filed, instead of dumping them in your out-box put them in a

TIP: SET A POSITIVE DEADLINE

Parkinson's Law states, "Work expands to fill time." Have you noticed how quickly you can get through papers on your desk just before you leave for a business trip or vacation? Or, if you have to get those expense reports done before you leave town, it's amazing how you can do so in less than an hour—but if you go into the office on Saturday to catch up, before you know it, the afternoon is over and the only thing you got done was the expense reports.

separate to-file box so you don't have to sort them again. You can go one step further and identify where you want them filed and write the file name or number in the upper right-hand corner. Then the actual filing will be simple enough that you can delegate it, or spend a lot less of your own time at it.

When I talk with prospective clients, they frequently ask, "How long will this take me?" My answer: "I'm not sure, but I do know that the longer you wait to begin, the longer it will take—and the more difficult it will be."

I Don't Know How

This reason is the least obvious to most people. Instead, they often criticize themselves for a lack of discipline ("I just don't have the stick-to-it-iveness" or "I get bored"). That may indeed be part of the problem, but usually the real problem is that they don't know what to do.

Roughly 95% of convention audience members raise a hand when I ask them, "How many of you wish you could manage your desk more effectively?" Yet almost no one raises a hand when I ask, "How many of you have taken a course in paper or computer-file management?" Fascinating—and discouraging—isn't it, that our educational systems and workplaces ignore such an essential skill?

← D. Wall

I Must Do It Perfectly

Perfectionism is one of the biggest stumbling blocks to

FROM MY FILES: THE TALE OF THE ROCKS

If you haven't already, I strongly recommend that you read Stephen Covey's book, *Seven Habits of Highly Successful People.* In it, he tells the story of the professor who stands in front of his class with a jar and some rocks. He puts the rocks in the jar and then asks, "Is it full?" The class answers "Yes," but he pulls out a box with some pebbles in it, and begins putting them in the jar. He then asks, "Is it full?" Catching on to him by this time, they answer, "Probably not." And he adds some sand, and final-ly, takes a pitcher of water and fills the jar to the top with the water.

"What is the lesson?" he asks. They answer with comments like "You can always get a little more done," or "Use little bits of time." "No, no," he replies. "The lesson is that you have to put in the rocks first or there won't be any room." That certainly is true when it comes to managing your desk. It's very easy to be frantically busy all day long, and come to the end of the day and realize you never got to your most important task.

effective organization. I often find a vestige of organization buried within a client's cluttered office, but it was a system too complicated to maintain. Instead of modifying a perfect system to make it possible and usable, the client abandoned it entirely to chaos.

Procrastination is an offshoot of perfectionism, one I know all too well. I experienced a revelation when I discovered that my perfectionism is the root of my continual temptation to procrastinate. If there's something I know I need to do, but I'm afraid I won't do it perfectly, and if I wait long enough to do it, then fear of not getting it done at all will overcome my fear of not doing it perfectly (got that?).

I Don't Want to Do It

That's a pretty straightforward reason for not getting organized, isn't it? But why not get organized?

A writer who had spent years in chaos finally decided she'd had enough. We spent hours sorting through boxes and piles from years past. Just as we were about to take the final step and put everything in order, she canceled her appointment. Years later she confessed to me that she realized she had always used her disorganization as an excuse for not being a productive writer. The fear

> ## TIP: ASSORTED EXCUSES
>
> Here are some common excuses for not getting organized
>
> - **My office** wouldn't stay organized anyway.
> - **Organizing** wouldn't make any difference.
> - **I have more important** things to do.
> - **I know where** everything is.
> - **Colleagues** would think that I didn't have enough work to do.

of not having that excuse paralyzed her.

The negative effects of one person's disorganization are multiplied at the company level and can often be assigned a dollar value. A large catering company had a very financially attractive lease on one of its kitchens, which stated that the company had to notify the building owner at the end of each year if it intended to renew the lease. When the staff member responsible for this obligation moved on, she left it as unfinished business and the catering company suffered a 100% rent increase.

Granted, it's not as exciting to file the papers from a completed project or contract as it was to complete the project. But the price we pay for not organizing the information can be high:

- **Missed deadlines** and resulting penalties.
- **Overlooked opportunities** and unrealized profits.
- **Time wasted** to recreate a paper trail when accountability is demanded and circumstances aren't fresh in anyone's memory.
- **Lost customers** because of poor service.
- **Increased cost** from poor use of physical—and human—resources.

But the greatest cost savings from organization may benefit you alone. Not only will organization save money, time and space, but it will also reduce your stress. As a result, your productivity and quality of life will improve.

TIP: DEFINE YOUR MISSION

Each of us has many different roles in our lives, competing for our time and attention. Sometimes all of these conflicting demands can make us lose sight of our goals, and paralyze us to the point where we can do nothing. This happens in business as well, and one way that businesses keep their goals clearly in sight is by developing a mission statement in which they identify their goals, as well as what's important and what's not. You can do the same.

I have found it enormously helpful to develop mission statements for both my personal and professional lives. I don't literally turn them into to-do lists. Instead, I use them as compasses to determine whether I'm going in the right direction: The clearer I am about what is most important to me, the clearer I am about what is important to do from among the tasks waiting for me.

In her book, *Life Is More Than Your To-Do List: Blending Business Success With Personal Satisfaction* (Bedrosian Communication Inc; 301-460-3408), author Maggie McAuliffe Bedrosian describes a discussion she once had with a reader about this subject. "The idea of a mission statement is too much for me," said the reader. "What can you suggest that's a little more down to earth?" Bedrosian replied, "If you can't give yourself a mission statement, could you at least give yourself a bumper sticker?" At its simplest, the mission statement should clearly and concisely summarize your life's purpose.

Here are my mission statements. I hope you find them helpful as guides for developing your own:

FOR BUSINESS

The purpose of the Hemphill Productivity Institute is to:

- **Encourage and assist** people and organizations to identify and implement organizing skills in order to increase productivity, reduce stress, and reach their personal and professional goals. Methods include speaking, training, consulting, and products.
- **Promote organizing** in order to improve quality of life and work in our society.
- **Provide the employees** and associates of Hemphill Productivity Institute with a healthy, supportive, and financially rewarding affiliation.
- **Provide financial rewards** to Barbara Hemphill to support a lifestyle that will allow her to continue the above indefinitely, and enable her to financially assist her extended family and other causes she deems worthy.
- **Serve God in all endeavors** with the hope that others will see His love through us.

FOR MY PERSONAL LIFE

I choose to feel and act satisfied, thankful, peaceful, loved and loving—in order to share God's love.

Don't Set Yourself Up With Unreal Expectations

A prospective client once called me for help. I discovered that she was required to work 60 hours a week. She had just moved to a new office, lost her secretary and been given a new computer system. On top of this she was a single parent caring for an ailing parent. Her problem wasn't lack of organization—it was a lack of reality. Given the demands on her time, she could never meet her own expectations or those of her employer.

If you make a to-do list day after day, never complete it, and feel continually stressed about it, it's time for a reality check. After you make the next day's list, estimate how long you'll need to complete each task. Add on a reasonable time for interruptions, and add up the time. Is your to-do list realistic?

In my younger, more naive, days I believed that if I just got organized enough and managed my time better, I could accomplish everything I wanted to.

Now, I cringe when I hear someone say, "You can always find time to do what you want to do." I now believe the truth is: "You can always find time to do what you want to do—if you're willing to give up something else." Life is a series of trade-offs. But nothing is forever, and it always amazes me that when I give up something temporarily, the time will come when it fits back into my life perfectly.

Deal With the Reality of Work

What if the to-do list that I created yesterday for today doesn't reflect today's realities? Many times it won't. That's one of the characteristics of our fast-moving society. It means that we constantly have to reevaluate our list, revising it and verifying it against our mission statements (see the box at left).

- **How do I handle today's crisis without completely forgetting my other priorities?** Weekly planning, weekly planning, weekly planning! (See the discussion beginning on page 62.)

- **Do I just put today's crisis at the top of the list and work my way down, as I can?** Ask, "What's the most important thing I need to do today?" Then begin doing it. When you get interrupted, handle the interruption, and go back to your priority. That may happen a dozen or more times every day.
- **What if I report to several people and they have conflicting priorities?** Good luck! Communication is the only answer I know. You may have to get your bosses together with you to discuss and negotiate their priorities for you. They may not even be aware that you're overwhelmed, and as long as you let them get away with it, they may find it convenient not to know; that way they won't have to reconsider their own priorities or those of their associates. Point out to your bosses that you're interested in getting their work done to the best of your ability and that working out priorities is the only way that can happen.

Eliminate To-Do's

You can begin to eliminate some items from your organizing to-do list by asking questions such as:

- **If I don't do this task, what's the worst possible thing that could happen?** Could I live with the consequences? If so, drop that item from your list.
- **Am I the only person who can do this?** If not, delegate the task.
- **Must this task be done now?** Can I put it off for a period of time and then reconsider its significance?
- **Is there a less complicated way to do it?** For example, instead of spending hours going through old files, can I pull out the ones I know I need to begin a new system, and put the others in less accessible space in case I need them?

Six Elements of Success

Even after you've identified what's important for you to organize, it's not always easy to do. Why? Organizing is a skill, and as with any other skill, developing it doesn't come without a price. If you wanted to be a tennis player, you could buy the best equipment, get the best coach, go to the best court, and play tennis for the weekend—but that wouldn't make you a good tennis player. You'd still have to invest plenty of time and energy in practicing and playing. The same is true for organizing. After you have identified what's important to organize, you must acquire or develop these six essential components to implement and maintain organization:

1. **Clear vision**
2. **Positive attitude**
3. **Sufficient time**
4. **Proper tools**
5. **Adequate skills**
6. **Ongoing maintenance**

Clear Vision

Organizing in and of itself has no value. It is simply a tool to help you do something that is important to you, such as spending less time looking for things, or making more money, or eliminating embarrassment when someone comes to your office. Seeing clearly the benefits of organizing will make the process go much more smoothly. One of the things I've discovered in 20 years as a professional organizer is that even the most disorganized people have organized some part of their lives—frequently one for which they have great passion. As a result, organizing it is much easier.

Positive Attitude

Positive attitude is key, for, as the saying goes, "Whether you think you can or think you can't, you're right."

Ironically, the success that comes from a positive attitude sometimes begets higher expectations that, in turn, diminish one's positive attitude. Years ago I walked into a client's office. All around the room papers were piled higher than my head. Every flat space was full. I had nowhere to sit. Files were too full to close. After several weeks of working together, the office looked good—and it worked.

Several years later my client called and apologized about the mess she had made. I somewhat fearfully re-

Whether you think you can or think you can't, you're right.

15

Many professionals now have offices at home, where one of the biggest challenges is having the right tools.

turned to her office. To my surprise and delight, I discovered a chair to sit on and plenty of evidence of organization. She had just waited too long for some routine maintenance. I reminded her of how things looked when I came in the first time. Her attitude about her organizing abilities was anything but positive, until she realized that the problem was now her decreased tolerance for clutter.

Sufficient Time

Time spent now is time saved—and sometimes money earned—in the long run. Let's say that you take 12 trips per year for an average of $1,000 in reimbursable expenses per trip. Suppose you normally take two hours to prepare your expense accounts for reimbursement, and you procrastinate such that you're without the money for a month longer than necessary. However, if you set up a system so that you can fill out your expense report while you're traveling and submit it immediately upon your return, and you deposit your reimbursement check into an account earning 4%, you'll earn an extra $40 in interest per year—not a lot, but the cost of a good meal in many cities. This practice will probably also improve your monthly cash flow. More importantly, instead of spending two hours trying to recreate your expenses when you get home (and feeling guilty for several hours before you actually get around to doing it), you can spend your time on something more productive.

The Right Tools

I grew up on a farm in Nebraska, and my father often told me, "Half of any job is having the right tool." The same principle applies in getting organized.

Let me illustrate this with an example from the home-office scene—it may be one you recognize: You come home and grab the mail. You want to have a cup of coffee while you read the mail, so instead of going to your office, you sit in the kitchen. You make piles—bills, payments, catalogs, personal and professional reading, a new assignment from your manager. There's plenty of stuff for the trash—but the trash can's on the other side of the room and you don't want to get up yet.

The phone rings—it's a colleague returning your call. You take notes at the kitchen table, after making the caller wait while you retrieve your prepared questions from the papers on the dining-room table. The kids come home from school, and by now you can't remember what's what, so you scoop it all up and put it in the bay window.

You repeat this scene several times that week. You have dinner guests on Saturday, so you shove all the papers into a drawer. A few days later, you realize you can't find the notes from your earlier conversation, and you've misplaced a source's phone number. Your manager calls to discuss the new assignment and you can't find that either. You search the house for the right pile and sort through it all over again.

Sound familiar? Then it's likely that a lack of tools is the major problem. Many professionals—self-employed and otherwise—now have offices at home. One of the biggest challenges of the home office is having the right tools—a designated space and everything from a telephone to a desk, from a filing system to the necessary computer software.

Whether you're organizing an office at home or away from home, this book will help you choose—and use—the tools that will help you get organized more effectively.

The Rest of the Game: Skills and Maintenance

If you have a clear vision of the value of being organized, and you're willing to accept that you can do it and to take the time to learn, this book will help you develop the skills, acquire the tools, and perform the maintenance. So let's get going.

CHAPTER 2

Let FAT Work for You

All those papers stacked up on your desk require decisions, as do your computer files and e-mail and voice-mail messages. But there's good news! You really have only three decisions you *can* make about any piece of information. You can:

- **File it.**
- **Act on it.**
- **Toss it.**

To make your choices easy to remember, think F-A-T (I call it the FAT System). This section will help you learn how to make those three key decisions quickly and well. To illustrate the process, I've developed a tool, the Information Management Flowchart, shown on page 22 of this chapter. It sounds heavy, but it's quite straightforward. The key word is flow. I've found that the problem isn't that too much information flows into an office—it's that too little flows out. Information in many forms gets stuck—and so do we! The difference between paper shuffling and paper management is decision making. You can use the FAT System and the flowchart to make decisions to take information from your in-basket—whether that's a box on your desk or files in your computer—and move it out.

The Art of Wastebasketry

I'm convinced that our ability to achieve goals is directly related to our willingness to use the wastebasket,

FROM MY FILES: OVERCOMING FEAR

People's fear of throwing things away is enormous. My seminar attendees frequently make statements such as, "Every time I throw something away, I need it again." When I challenge them to elaborate, their response is often, "I can't think of an example right now." Whether they're experiencing the fear of failing to be knowledgeable in their field of expertise or the fear of failing to produce information when asked to by a superior, the results are the same: overstuffed filing cabinets and hard drives. For 15 years I have orchestrated File Clean-Out Days for companies (see Chapter 16). I used to have nightmares that after such an event an attendee would call me with a horror story about something that they threw away and later needed. It has never happened.

whether it's the circular file next to your desk or the trash can icon on your computer. I've no doubt that your stress level will decrease as the amount of stuff in your wastebasket increases.

It's not practical—or perhaps even possible—to keep everything that arrives in your office. When you run out of space or can't find what you need—on your desk or in your computer—life becomes unbearable.

And, besides, Hemphill's Principle states: If you don't know you have it, or you can't find it, it is of no value to you.

Fear of Throwing Out

Why is it so difficult to use the wastebasket?

- **Habit.** People get in the habit of just looking through their mail to see what is there, without throwing out all unwanted mail immediately.
- **Lack of focus.** If I'm not sure what information is important, it's tough to figure out what to toss.
- **Fear.** The what-if game can go on endlessly: What if someone asks me about this, and I don't have it? What if I don't know everything that is in this publication? What if next week I decide I want it?

Logic-Based Disposal

You can overcome those impediments by using logic-based disposal. Determine whether you want to keep each piece of paper by asking yourself these Art of Wastebasketry questions:

Does this require any action on my part? Just because you receive information—even if it's from your boss—doesn't mean you need to keep it. (She may just be cleaning off her desk.) If it doesn't require action, file it or toss it away. If it's just an FYI, read it and toss.

Does this exist elsewhere? Is it in the library? Do you know an expert on the subject who'd be certain to have more complete information if you really needed it? Is the original in a file elsewhere? Do you also have a book or manual on the same subject? Is it necessary to keep a hard copy if it exists in the computer? Could you just bookmark the item on your Internet browser?

Is this information recent enough to be useful? Today, information becomes outdated very quickly. Would you want a customer to decide whether to choose your services on the basis of a three-year-old brochure? The information in a six-month-old magazine article about computer software has undoubtedly been superseded, as has a product review downloaded from an online service. In many cases, rather than keeping the information itself, it is more appropriate to keep track of the *source* of the information, so that you can get the latest version whenever you need it.

Can I identify specific circumstances when I'd use this information? Usually, "just in case" is not specific enough. Files labeled Miscellaneous are of little value, because there's no clue to trigger you to look there. If you can't identify how you'd use the information—at least well enough that you can label the file for future reference—it's unlikely that you'd remember you have it, let alone be able to find it later.

Are there any tax or legal implications? Here's where "just in case" works. Unfortunately, we may be re-

TOOL: INFORMATION-MANAGEMENT FLOWCHART

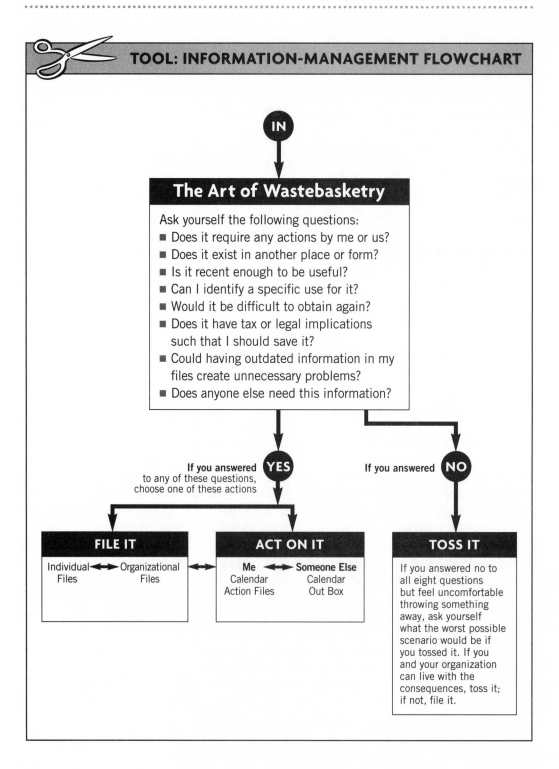

IN

The Art of Wastebasketry

Ask yourself the following questions:
- Does it require any actions by me or us?
- Does it exist in another place or form?
- Is it recent enough to be useful?
- Can I identify a specific use for it?
- Would it be difficult to obtain again?
- Does it have tax or legal implications such that I should save it?
- Could having outdated information in my files create unnecessary problems?
- Does anyone else need this information?

If you answered YES to any of these questions, choose one of these actions

If you answered NO

FILE IT

Individual ◄► Organizational
Files   Files

ACT ON IT

Me ◄► **Someone Else**
Calendar   Calendar
Action Files   Out Box

TOSS IT

If you answered no to all eight questions but feel uncomfortable throwing something away, ask yourself what the worst possible scenario would be if you tossed it. If you and your organization can live with the consequences, toss it; if not, file it.

quired to resurrect paper that we'd much rather have forgotten—say, in an IRS audit (see Chapter 17).

Could having outdated information in my files create unnecessary problems? A client of mine was sued, and the company's files were subpoenaed. One of the files contained a copy of a contract that had never been executed. The prosecuting attorney was able to use that document to prove that my client's intent was wrongful, and the company lost the suit. If the files had been properly cleaned, I don't believe that would have happened.

Does anyone else need this information? This is a critical question, but in many organizations people neither know the answer nor where to get it. The discussion of Retention Guidelines, below, will help you get the answer.

What is the worst possible thing that could happen if I did not have this information? If you have answered no to the preceding questions, but are still not comfortable throwing something away, this question becomes key. If you're willing to live with the results of throwing something out, toss it. If not, keep it.

How you answer this question is significant in determining your retention philosophy, which I'll discuss in a moment. Two people might initially answer this way: "The worst possible thing that could happen is that someone would get upset with me." However, one of the two might continue with, "I'll risk it!" and throw away the item, while the other would say, "It's not worth the risk!" and keep it. Neither person's approach is right or wrong; each one simply reflects a different tolerance for risk.

Retention Guidelines

I was originally motivated to write my first book, *Taming the Paper Tiger at Home,* in an effort to answer the question, "How long do I keep…?"

When I began organizing businesses, I discovered that document retention is a far bigger issue at the office than at home. Frequently, the reason file cabinets overflow and computer disks seem to multiply is that

TIP: ORGANIZING OVERVIEW

When your desk—and your life—begins to feel out of control, remember: There are only three actions you can take on any piece of paper: toss it, file it, or act on it. The following chapters will discuss each of these steps, and more, in detail. But it's not too soon to get a sense of the whole ball game. Here are the steps you'll be following:

1. Make sure that you can sit comfortably at your desk and easily reach your waste-basket, in-box, out-box and to-file box (see the discussion of your in-box on page 26, the list of essential office supplies on pages 28–29, and Chapter 4).

2. Divide all the papers that you decide to keep as follows:
- Reference files contain information that you may want or need at some point in the future, whereas
- Action files contain information for current tasks or projects.

3. Identify an easily accessible place for action papers, perhaps on top of your desk or in a drawer (see pages 83–84 in Chapter 8).

4. Make a list of existing reference files. File titles should clearly indicate the contents. Put papers in their largest general category first and break them down into smaller categories when the files get too bulky (see Chapter 4).

5. Consider creating a library file for articles that you'd like to read (see page 80).

6. Save your most accessible space for your regular reference files, those that you will consult most frequently, and separate out files that you need for historical or archival purposes and put them in a less-accessible space.

7. Organize all non-paper items into like categories: books, computer documentation, diskettes, supplies, and so on. Use adhesive notes to temporarily label them while you are organizing.

8. Label a container or shelf for each category of item. When the space is filled, find a larger container or space.

9. If Item A and Item B belong together, but you can find only one or the other, ask yourself, "Where would I put this if I had both pieces?" Put away whatever you can find now, and eventually you'll get the two pieces together.

10. Keep asking:
- Do I really need or want this?
- What is the worst possible thing that would happen if I didn't have it?
- What's the next action I need to take?
- If I wanted to find this again, what words would I think of first?
- Where can I put it so that I can find it when I'm ready for it?

no one has made decisions about what should and should not be kept—and for how long.

People often refuse to make these decisions because they're certain there's one right answer; as soon as they discover what it is, they'll begin to purge. Even if you consult five authorities about retention guidelines for records, you may get several different answers. You're the only person who can make the final decision.

My experience is that the more organized we get, the more willing we are to let go. But in the case of business papers, it's important to determine what we must keep to protect ourselves and our organization and to carry out those decisions. In the case of an audit or lawsuit, failing to have or to carry out such guidelines appears sloppy at best and fraudulent at worst.

Set Up Your Own Guidelines

First, check with your organization to see what retention guidelines already exist. Many companies have them, but don't do a good job of communicating them to their employees, and everyone is left to figure out the rules for themselves. It's just as bad to have rules that are not user-friendly. Here are a few ways to start building retention guidelines. (If you're the boss, you'll find discussion in Chapter 15 about how to effectively communicate these guidelines to your employees.)

To learn about any legal, tax or financial issues, as it relates to retention, first check with your boss, general counsel or accountant. If you don't get a satisfactory answer from your employer, then check the resources shown in the box on page 174 of Chapter 17.

Check with your professional or trade association to see what retention guidelines it can provide. While it's worth asking, it is interesting to note that most associations don't have retention guidelines, even though such guidelines could prevent their members from having to reinvent the wheel.

If you're new to a job, don't act immediately. Say that

> For every hour of organizing, allow 10 minutes for picking up loose ends—emptying trash, putting away supplies, and so on.

you've inherited file drawers of someone else's stuff and you must create your own retention guidelines. In that case, it will take a year before you can determine what to keep or dispose of, so put the old stuff in an out-of-the-way place until you can decide. Then, reflect on your actual experience with the records you are keeping. Ask yourself:

- **How far back** in the records have you actually gone to retrieve information?
- **What would happen** if you didn't have those records? Would you or your organization suffer any legal consequences?

Determine a good place to put retention guidelines. A clearly labeled notebook—or a section of a procedures manual, if there is one—would work. My favorite place to put my retention guidelines is on my File Index, a comprehensive listing of all my files (see the discussion of File Indexes, with a sample index on pages 48–52).

Identify What's Important by Eliminating What's Not

As I constantly remind my clients, *how* you organize is not nearly as important as *what* you organize. No doubt you could effectively manage every piece of paper on your desk and every file in your computer if that was all you had to do—but it isn't. So the real question becomes, What can I ignore?

Your In-Box

For many people, the in-box—for paper or electronic stuff—is a holding pen for postponed decisions. You shuffle through it and don't know what to do with every item, or don't feel like figuring it out. So those items go back in the box and you shuffle them for a few more weeks, along with the new material that arrives.

The real purpose of the in-box is to physically separate items you haven't looked at from those you have. Let's say that you sit down at your desk to look at today's

TIP: MANAGING STORAGE CLOSETS

Storage closets are a sore spot in many offices. I can't tell you how often I've heard a frustrated client say, "I just organized that last week, and it's a mess already." Here are some tips that will help:

- **Make sure that you have the right equipment** for what you're trying to store. For example, boxes of files may need fewer (but heavily reinforced and deep) shelves, while small office supplies, such as pens and staples, will probably need more shelves, but not necessarily stronger ones.

- **Figure out the maximum quantity** of each item that you want to have on hand and allow enough room for it.

- **Put small items,** such as pens, labels, staples, and so on, in small containers to keep them from being scattered everywhere.

- **Clearly label all shelves** and containers so that everyone knows where to find what they need and to put things back where they found them.

- **Develop a simple system**—one they'll actually use and that is easily maintained—for users to indicate when supplies are low. Consider posting a supply checklist and pen on or near the closet door.

- **Assign someone** to regularly maintain the storage closet.

mail, which you put in the center of your desk. You get part way through and the phone rings—or someone stops by your office—and you need to find a file to get information. Another interruption follows. Before you know it, your desk is covered with papers you have looked at and papers you haven't. Now you have to sort through them all over again, which simply wastes time.

In-box to the rescue. Instead of putting the papers in the middle of your desk, leave them in the in-box—until you're prepared to do something with each piece that you remove.

You have probably heard the advice, Handle a piece of paper only once. Many people try that and fail, so they give up. Let's adapt that strategy a little: Handle a piece of paper only once—after you've taken it out of your in-box. Use the in-box to hold items that you haven't looked at yet. Once you've removed something from the in-box, remember the FAT principle—file, act or toss—then handle it once to make one of these decisions. You can then put the item in a specific

TOOL: A LIST OF ESSENTIALS

In Chapter 1, I discussed the importance of having the right tool, and certainly office supplies fall into that category. For example, nothing is more frustrating than clipping a magazine article for your files, and when you go to staple it, discovering that you are out of staples. At that point you can waste time making a special trip to get staples, interrupt a colleague to borrow some, or fold the page corners together, only to have them fall apart. Wouldn't it be simpler to just make sure you have an extra box of staples?

Here's a checklist of office supplies that every well-organized office should have:

Boxes
- In-box for items you haven't looked at
- Out-box for items to be mailed or delivered to someone else
- To-file box for items to be filed in drawers you can't reach from your chair

Calendar—paper or electronic
Card file and extra cards for contact information, unless you prefer to manage such information electronically on your computer or personal digital assistant (PDA).

Clock

Desk tools, including:
- Ruler
- Magnifying glass for reading fine print
- Scissors

Disposal tools, including:
- Paper shredder (see page 156)
- Trash can
- Recycling bin

Fasteners, including:
- Rubber bands
- Paper clips and binder clips
- Stapler and staple remover
- Tape and tape dispenser

place, such as a to-file box or an Action File (see Chapter 8), so that when it's time for you to take appropriate action, you'll know exactly where to look for it.

With mail, paper or electronic, take immediate action—especially tossing or deleting—whenever possible. If you're more comfortable managing paper, print out e-mail messages that require action, and handle them as you would any piece of paper (see Chapter 8).

Any Backlog

It's a big mistake to think that the way to "get this office organized" is to start with the backlog. Guess what happens when you start that way? While you're working on

Labelmaker. You may want this for labeling files, shelves and doors.

Postage meter and scale. If your office doesn't have a mailroom or you're working from home and send mail out frequently, this will save you time at the post office. For small mailings, you can buy an adequate postage scale. For larger mailings, you may want to rent a postage meter scale from Pitney Bowes (800-672-6937; www.pitneybowes.com).

Stationery supplies. Even if you're working in a totally electronic environment, there still may be occasions when you will need to send something by conventional postal or freight delivery. In that case, you need not overinvest in these items, but just keep a few of them on hand:
- Address and return-address labels
- Adhesive notes
- Business stationery and envelopes
- Envelopes of various sizes
- File folders and labels
- Notecards
- Postcards

Writing utensils including:
- Container for them, unless you'd rather keep them in your desk drawer
- Felt-tipped pen for handwriting file labels
- Highlighter
- Pens in different colors for making calendar notations
- Thick marker for marking boxes

last week's stuff, today's information pours in. Unless you deal with it right away, it becomes next week's backlog. You get bogged down and give up.

Start by putting the most recent papers in your in-box—today's mail as well as papers that require action. Put the old papers in a box under your desk, or in a bottom drawer. If you need something fairly recent, you'll know to dig through the in-box; it's less likely that you'll need something from the old pile—if you had, it would have risen to the top of the heap already—but you can still find what you need. As time allows, you can pull papers out of the old pile and merge them into your new system. The old papers will be easier to han-

TIP: BEFORE YOU BEGIN

Things often get worse before they get better. This is a natural and unavoidable consequence of beginning to get organized. This is not the time to go get a cup of coffee or chat with your neighbor.

If a component of your system is weak or missing, the system will break down, which frequently indicates a changing focus. I guarantee that a change in your job, such as a promotion, increase or reduction in support staff, relocation, or travel will require you to restructure or rearrange your system.

When you are tempted to defer deciding on the fate of an item, ask yourself: What will I know tomorrow that I don't know now? If you will know more at a later date, put the paper in your Pending File to await action once you have complete information. Also, put a reminder on the appropriate date in your calendar to look in your Pending File (see pages 80-81 of Chapter 8 for more on this). Use the same process for e-mail or voice-mail messages and faxes.

Continually ask yourself: Does my organizing system still work for me? Do I still like it? And, if your system affects others, ask: Does it work for them?

dle anyway once you've set up a system you understand, and in many cases, you'll probably be able to throw them away. We'll describe how to set up a filing system later on.

File It to Find It

Let's go back to the Information Management Flowchart, on page 22. If you're unwilling to live with the consequences of tossing out information, you have two options: File it or act on it.

I've discovered that if a client's desk is a major disaster in terms of the amount of paper piled on it, the filing system probably doesn't work. Clients would file much of the information they receive—if they knew they could find it again when they need it. If they're not sure that's the case, they figure it's safer just to leave the material in a heap on their desks.

But think of it this way: Often, a filing system is to an organization what a foundation is to a building. You can get away with a poorly constructed foundation for a while. You can put a fancy building on top, and lavishly decorate the interior, but sooner or later the foundation will crumble and the building will fall.

Today, information is power. If we don't have the right information at the right time, we lose opportunities. Therefore, if the filing system isn't working, our company may fall—or at least falter.

Keep in mind that the value of an effective filing system is that you can retrieve information when you need it—it's not just a place for storage. The purpose of filing anything—paper or electronic—is to create a place to put the information so that you will be able to find it again—easily. Bottom-line, think, "Where can I find this," instead of "Where can I put this?"

PART 2

Getting Started

CHAPTER 3

The Mechanics of Filing Paper

Do you hate filing? A major corporation did an extensive survey on the most hated job in the office. You won't be surprised to find that the result was filing. But you can reduce stress if you know where to put a piece of paper or a computer file, so you can find it when you want it. And that requires a filing system.

I've never met anyone who could successfully organize an office without also using a filing system—or without working with someone who actually does the filing. Yet, I'm continually surprised at how few people really know how to create and maintain a system that works. Frequently, the problem is the mechanics of the system, and a little change can make a big difference in the success of its use.

Consider one of my clients, a social-services office. I walked in and found piles of files on top of file cabinets. Apparently, the practice was to create a new-client file in green. When the case was closed, the file was put in a blue folder. Unfortunately, the same client often reappeared with a new problem—sometimes while the original file was still on top of the cabinet waiting for its new colored file, making it really difficult to find the necessary file.

The solution? It was simple: We decided that all client files would be green. Open cases and closed cases were filed alphabetically by client name in separate cabinets. This system required only a simple move of files between cabinets with no filing-system glitches to hang anyone up.

Filing Tools: Decisions That Make a Difference

A Filing Cabinet

I can't overemphasize the importance of high-quality equipment. You may be better off buying used filing cabinets, which may be sturdier than new, but poorer-quality, ones. A consultant purchased some old but excellent-quality cabinets from a government agency for $50 each. For another $50, she hired an appliance-painting company to paint them bright red—to match her office counter tops. Here are some other purchasing pointers:

Make certain you get a good-quality, full-suspension cabinet. Full-suspension means that you can pull out the drawers all the way so that no files are obstructed from your view, and you can open only one drawer at a time so that the cabinet will not tip over. These cabinets come in many styles and colors to complement your decor and available space.

You'll have a choice of a vertical or lateral file. If you're short on wall space, you may want a higher, but narrower, vertical file cabinet. If you want additional work or counter space in your area, consider a two-drawer lateral file cabinet, which is shorter and wider. The top of the lateral file can hold your printer, fax machine or working files.

Lateral files are typically arranged so that when you pull a drawer out, the files and file names face sideways. That may work for you if your lateral files are positioned to either side of your usual seated position, from which you will usually pull out the drawer to consult your files. But what if you're most likely to use the files while facing them? Most lateral drawers are designed so that you can add metal bars in the center of the drawer and arrange your files in two side-by-side rows that face you.

Open-Shelf Filing

An option that most people overlook is open-shelf filing—

the kind you've probably seen used in doctors' offices. Shelf filing goes up the wall, rather than out from the wall. It can save you a considerable amount of space and money. According to Advanced Office Systems, a filing supplier, use of open-shelf filing can reduce use of floor space use by 60% at about one-third of the cost of conventional filing methods.

There are people who find traditional filing systems of cabinets and files unworkable—they simply prefer cubbyholes and piles. These people may want to consider using either open shelves divided into compartments or collapsible cardboard dividers, which hold the equivalent of one ream of paper and can be purchased from an office-supply company. These systems will work for someone who likes their material divided into large categories of information, as opposed to lots of smaller categories. For example, let's take all the information you have about your office equipment. That would make one large category appropriate for the cubbyhole or pile method. If, however, you prefer to divide the information into subcategories—such as computer equipment, telephone equipment, and so on—a system of compartments would require a large amount of space and you'd probably be better off using a traditional filing system.

Tabletop Tools for Action Files

Later on in the book, we'll cover information, such as current topics or projects, for which you may create special files—which, appropriately, are called Action Files. For these, you may want a wire rack or portable plastic file holder that sits on the top of your desk or credenza for easy access. If you have file drawers under your desk, you might want to designate one drawer for Action Files (see Chapter 8).

File Folders

Unless you've got a substantial amount of legal-size paper, I recommend letter-size file folders. They take less space, cost less money, and because they're smaller they're easier to handle.

People who prefer cubbyholes and piles may want to consider using either open shelves divided into compartments or collapsible cardboard dividers.

TIP: THE PORTABLE FILING BOX

One of the best organizing tools on the market is the portable filing box. These boxes come in a variety of styles and prices and can be used to create an office in a small space. In anticipation of working with clients who have no file space and with whom they need to create an immediate impact by filing desk papers, our company's consultants always carry portable filing boxes in their cars. I use one in the cubbyhole beneath my desk for temporary projects that generate large amounts of paper, such as chairing a committee or preparing my taxes.

HANGING FILES. For Reference Files (those containing material you will want at some future date), I prefer hanging files. These are a sort of sling for file folders, suspended from a frame in the file drawer that allows you to slide them back and forth in the cabinet, giving you better access and preventing interior files within from sliding down and disappearing in a loosely filled drawer. I recommend hanging files that are reinforced and have "info pockets" for holding business cards, small pieces of paper and computer diskettes.

If your file cabinet doesn't accommodate hanging files, you can purchase a hanging-file frame that you can size to fit the file drawer.

INTERIOR FILES. I'm often asked "How do you know when to put a manila file in the hanging file?" Actually, the file you would use inside a hanging file is called an interior file. These look like traditional manila file folders, but they are slightly shorter, so that they don't stick up so far in the hanging files. They come in a variety of colors. My guidelines for using interior folders are simple:

- **If the hanging file will remain in the cabinet,** and you're only going to take out the piece of paper you need, do not use an interior file.
- **If you would otherwise remove the entire hanging file**—such as one dedicated to a project, a commit-

---

TIP: TOO LARGE FOR A FILE

If you need to store numerous oversized items, such as artwork or posters, purchase a file cabinet designed for that purpose (sometimes known as a flat file). If you lack special accommodations for such items, place a note in the file where the material would have been placed if it had fit, indicating where you have stored it (for example, "behind supply cabinet" or "on third shelf in division director's office").

---

tee, or a client—then use interior files inside the hanging file. Make sure to label the two types of files identically. This will make it easy for you or someone else to return the interior file to its proper place in the hanging file.

- **In some cases,** you may want to use interior files to make subdivisions in a hanging file. For example, the hanging folder could be labeled "Annual Meeting" and the interior folders labeled "Annual Meeting: 2003," "Annual Meeting: 2002," and so on. Make certain that you put the major heading, not just the year, on the interior file so it will be refiled properly if removed from the hanging file. (If you use a numerical system with *Kiplinger's Taming the Paper Tiger* software, putting the number on the file on the interior folder will make re-filing into the hanging file a snap.)

BOX-BOTTOM HANGING FILES. This type of file has a cardboard strip in the bottom, ranging from a half-inch to 3 inches in width, that will support files that are very thick or have many subdivisions. Make sure you choose a size slightly smaller than or equivalent to the thickness of the material you are filing. If you put 2 inches of material in a 3-inch file, the material will fold over and the file will not hang properly.

END-TAB FILE FOLDERS FOR SHELVES. If you opt for open-shelf filing or use traditional bookshelves for filing, you'll need specially designed end-tab shelf-file folders. On conventional file folders, the labeling tab appears on the top of the file folder. On end-tab file folders, the labeling tab appears on the end of the folder that will face out from the shelf. These come in a multitude of styles, shapes and colors.

Labeling Your Files: The Key to an Effective Filing System

Here are some tips that will help you make the most of your filing system:

Start by putting plastic tabs on the front or opening edge of hanging files. Then, no matter how full a hanging file gets, you'll still be able see its label. In addition, when you go to file, you can grab the plastic tab and pull it toward you, creating a space to put the paper and automatically arranging the papers chronologically with the most recent in front. To purge your files quickly, simply pull out the oldest papers from the back of the files.

Stagger the labels across the tops of the hanging files so that you can read all of them without having to move files when you open a drawer. When you add a new file, you needn't change all the labels so that they are staggered in order. Just place the new label so that it doesn't sit immediately in front or back of another file label.

If you use interior files, put file names as close to the top of the file tabs as possible so that they will be more easily visible in the file drawer.

If you use peel-and-stick labels with a color edge on one side, place the label with the color on the bottom and the words at the top. It will be easier to read the labels.

If the label must be typed, handwrite a temporary label. Presuming that the label indeed must be typed (are you sure?), this will help you avoid procrastinating. Then you or someone else can go back and make the proper label.

If you use *Kiplinger's Taming the Paper Tiger* software, labels are included with the package, and you can print out additional ones to fit your needs.

If you're the only one using the files and you don't have to live up to anyone else's standards or meet their needs, simply handwrite your label with a felt-tip pen. You'll have no reason to procrastinate.

Colored Files and Labels: Use Them to Good Advantage

Thank goodness the days of drab green hanging files and manila files are gone. Colored files and labels are wonderful for livening up your office and can provide very practical cues for visually oriented people. However, unless you want to use your favorite color for all your files and your supply cabinet is consistently stocked with the same color of files, use color only when it tells a story worth telling—and then sparingly. For example, it might make sense for your Administrative Files to be one color, project files a second color, and personnel files a third color. If you're not sure about using color, begin by using one color. You can always add color later by adding colored dots on the labels.

I used the latter approach in an academic publisher's office that had files for editors of various subjects. There was a separate system for each subject, such as English, Spanish and Math, within which the editors' files were arranged alphabetically by their last names. Things got complicated when the secretary needed to find a file for an editor whose subject she didn't know or who worked in more than one subject. We simplified the system by filing all editors' files alphabetically by last name, assigning a different colored dot to each subject and applying the appropriate dots to each editor's file label. So if an editor worked in three subjects, for example, the secretary would put three, different-colored dots on the file. If the secretary needed to find all the math editors, she could pull all the files with red dots.

Use color only when it tells a story worth telling—and then sparingly.

Filing Made Easier

The following general tips will make the mechanics of your paper filing easier:

Avoid using paper clips. They catch on papers when you file them, taking those papers with them and possibly losing them forever, as well as obstructing file labels. Paper clips make for thicker files than staples. It's better to staple together related papers, and keep a staple remover handy for separating them as necessary.

Put the most recent papers in the front of the file. Whenever you reopen the file, you'll see the latest information or most recent action. Cleaning out files will be easier, because you will know that the oldest papers are at the back of the file.

Arrange file folders alphabetically (or numerically if you're using *Kiplinger's Taming the Paper Tiger* software. I've found that many people resist alphabetical filing because their files are stuffed with things they never use, and they'd rather have their most important files in the front of the drawer. But if you eliminate unnecessary paper from your filing system, you'll be amazed at how quickly you'll find an alphabetically-filed file. Also, if you're out of the office, associates will find it easy to find the files they need.

Don't file envelopes unless the postmark date is significant. Use your card file or contact manager program to record return addresses (see Chapters 5 and 6).

Date the papers that you file. Dating everything will help you or someone else know when it's time to seek updated information and toss out the old.

Stamp "File Copy: Do Not Remove" when appropriate. For example, stamp one copy of your company newsletter, a resource directory used by the entire department, or the last copy of a form. If you'll need additional pho-

TIP: SCANNING DOCUMENTS

A variety of new scanning products are available to help you eliminate paper from your office. For some kinds of paper in some circumstances, these scanning devices are highly desirable. But many of my clients have tried them with limited success. Either the paper they have doesn't lend itself to scanning—or they simply don't have time for this task. Some clients have simply added to-scan piles to their office clutter—right next to their to-read pile.

Wherever you choose to store your files, remember that simply filing papers out of sight is a waste of time. The key to an effective system is to properly identify each file before you put it away so that you can find it easily when you need it. I'll discuss ways to label files in Chapter 4, where I'll also describe *Kiplinger's Taming the Paper Tiger* software, a numerical labeling and retrieval system.

tocopies, don't waste space keeping a sheaf of copies on hand; instead, put one copy in a plastic cover to keep it clean and make copies as you need them.

Allow at least 3 inches of extra space in the cabinet for easier filing and retrieval. You know how difficult it is to find something when a file drawer is so crammed you can barely get a finger in the file. When setting up a new system, leave 20% of each drawer empty to allow for growth.

Label the outside of each file drawer with removable tape. Describe the drawer's contents either by subject or alphabetically (for example, "Financial Records" or "General Files, A-Mc").

Keep a to-file box or pile—separate from your out-box—near your desk. Many of the papers that arrive in your in-box simply need to be filed. By putting them directly in the to-file box you'll minimize the clutter on your desk.

Write a key word (or file number) in the upper-right-hand corner of the paper when you put it in your to-file box. It's easier to make filing decisions when you've just read the letter or article, and the filing task will be sim-

FROM MY FILES: CARD-FILE PLUS

A television producer eliminated a large file drawer of materials by making better use of her card file. For example, instead of keeping a file thick with materials about Alzheimer's disease, she substituted one file card labeled "Alzheimer's," which noted the names, Web sites, and telephone numbers of three Alzheimer's experts. Those experts were more likely to give her the most current information and contacts than a bunch of old newspaper and magazine clippings.

pler because you've already identified where to put the paper. This method is essential if someone else does your filing, because no two people would necessarily put a paper in the same file.

CHAPTER 4

Set Up Your File System

O kay, you've assembled the necessary tools, and you've got a full to-file box. All those papers have to go somewhere, so it's time to build your system.

Here are some tips to help you design a filing system that will work for you. You'll find that, in principle, much of this advice will apply to how you manage your computer files as well (a subject that is further discussed in Chapter 9).

Keep Your System Simple

O ne of the biggest temptations—and most frequent mistakes—is to create too many systems (referred to as "locations" if you use *Taming the Paper Tiger* software; see page 48). Suppose you have a job in which you wear several hats. Your first inclination may be to set up a separate system for each role, but you'll run into trouble if the information you use overlaps. If you're looking for something, you'll first have to remember which filing system it's in, and then where it is within the system. When you're filing, you may find it difficult to determine which system is appropriate for that particular piece of information.

I use a technique that greatly helps me in determining when to start a new system: If you have any question as to how many systems you should have and what they should be, begin by putting all of the files together in one system, alphabetically. Then, if you are looking for brochure information you will go directly to

It's better to put information into the largest general category first. It's easier to go through one file with 20 pieces of paper than through ten files with two papers each.

"B," instead of wondering whether you put it in the subject files or the project files.

If one category in the system becomes large enough to fill half a drawer, consider creating a separate system. For example, let's say your company decides to implement a new customer-service program. In the beginning, perhaps one file will be enough, but, as the program is implemented and expands, more and more files will become necessary. At that point, you can pull together all the files related to customer service and put them in a separate drawer, filed alphabetically.

File According to Its Use, Not Its Source

A speaker at your annual convention impressed you, and you'd like to invite her to speak at a local event. You could file her handout under "Speaker Ideas" or "Regional Seminar Planning" rather than "Annual Convention." Or a brochure that you think is well-designed and could serve as an example of how you'd like to design your next brochure could be filed under "Brochure Ideas" rather than "Services" or the name of the company represented in the brochure.

Fewer Places to Look, Fewer Places to Lose

Most filing systems have too many files. It's easier to go through one file with 20 pieces of paper than through ten files with two papers each. It's better to put information into the largest general category first. Then if that file becomes too bulky, break it down. However, in rare instances, if an important document could not easily be found in any existing file, then it may merit a separate file. You could, for example, file your passport with other personal papers in a file labeled "Personal," but it's probably more helpful to have a document of that importance in a separate file, called "Passport." (With *Taming the*

Paper Tiger software, simply adding the key word "passport" to a file called "Personal Records" will enable you to find it in a few seconds, regardless of where you filed it.)

See Also . . .

I get lots of questions about cross-referencing files. If a document applies to more than one file, you can make a copy for the second, or to avoid excessive duplication, you can simply place a note on or inside the second file. "See also . . ." written on the file folder itself will frequently be adequate.

In reality, cross-referencing takes more time than most people are willing to give. Here's where creating a filing tool called the File Index will solve the problem. With a File Index, you can quickly scan a list of all the file names in your system and pick out the places where the document could have been filed. We'll discuss creating a File Index in just a moment.

Fix the System or Start Over?

I f you have a filing system that's not working well, or if you inherited it from someone else—whether the system is in your file cabinet or in your computer—it's usually best to start over. It will be easier to find what you want when you need it if you have one filing system that works for you, even if it's a small one—say, just a few files as you start.

Starting over doesn't mean days of purging old files and creating new ones. Instead, as you take documents from the old system and use them, refile them in the new system. Eventually the two systems will merge into one, or the old one will become so outdated that you'll feel comfortable throwing the remainder of it away. The same approach applies to creating a new computer filing system.

When you take a new job, chances are you won't be given a copy of the company's information-retention guidelines, and it may take a year before you will be able to decide what you must keep and what you can toss. If

> **As you take documents from the old system and use them, refile them in the new system. Eventually the old and new systems will merge into one.**

TIP: *KIPLINGER'S TAMING THE PAPER TIGER* SOFTWARE

About the only thing that technology has not changed in our office so far is the filing cabinet, which looks much as it did in Thomas Jefferson's office. What has changed is that there are more of them and they're in worse shape. Ironically, those cabinets—where many people can't find what they want at all—often sit right next to a computer where they can get information from the other side of the world in minutes.

I've taken advantage of the computer's ability to retrieve information quickly to create *Kiplinger's Taming the Paper Tiger* software (for additional information about the program, call 800-430-0794, or visit www.thepapertiger.com). With it, you can keep the paper you like and use your computer to find it in seconds—literally. In addition, filing paper takes a fraction of the time.

The concept is very simple. Instead of struggling to figure out what words you can fit on a file label that will help you find a piece of paper again, you identify the file folder with a random number. In your computer, you name the paper in as many ways as you like. Searching the File Index by any one of those names will point the user to the randomly numbered file. As a result, your papers will be automatically cross-referenced so that you—or anyone else—can find what you need. If the thought of having your files in random order is frightening, think about this: In a traditional filing system, we group files together—not because we need them together, but because it's the only way we could find them. Using the software to find your files is similar to searching for information on the Internet—you don't care where it comes from as long as you get it. In addition, if you're afraid to file a piece of paper because you'll forget to look at it, you can enter an action date, and the software will automatically remind you to look at your file.

You can print out an alphabetical list of your file names and keywords, and other helpful reports and file labels, too.

in doubt, keep it. Just leave it in the old filing system until you're sure you won't need it.

The File Index:
Your Key to Success

The main reason that filing systems break down is that you can file the same information under different names. Take auto information—you can file it under "Auto," "Car," "Chrysler," or "Vehicle." If several people use the same files, someone will inevitably file or refile similar material under different headings. Even if you're the only person using the file, it's easy to forget what word you used the first time.

The File Index, a list of the names of all the files in your filing system, is a crucial tool that serves two major purposes:

- **It will help you decide whether to fix up your existing system,** or start over. If you find that you know what few of the file titles mean, it may be easier to start over. On the other hand, if you know what the titles mean, but in some cases you think another label would be more useful or that a file needs to be located someplace else, you can probably just rearrange your existing system.
- **After you've set up a system, you can avoid making essentially duplicate files.** For example, a file for "Car" isn't necessary when your File Index shows that you already have one for "Vehicle."

To start your File Index, make a list of your existing files. That's an easy two-person job. One person reads off the names of the files, and the other one types it into a word-processing file.

Look at the list:

- **Does the file title tell you exactly what's inside?** If most of the file titles are mysterious, start a new system.
- **Are the titles descriptive,** but some overlap, such as "Car" and "Vehicle?" Or perhaps there's an occasional file title that doesn't clearly describe what's in the file. In those cases, revise the File Index itself and make the physical files match the index.

By the way, if the person who decides what can and can't be purged from the files won't come near them, the File Index is a great way to get the decision made. You can give the decision-maker a copy and ask for input. He or she need only review the list of files with your recommendations. You can make notes by the file names such as, "I've been here for two years, and we've never used this," "Accounting keeps this in their office," or "Contains info from 1987."

TOOL: BARBARA HEMPHILL'S FILE INDEX AT WORK

Here is an excerpt from the Hemphill Productivity Institute's File Index.

Administration and General Information:
Yellow Files—Lateral File Drawers #1-3
March 3, 2002

26	Advertising Published	102	Better Business Bureau
97	AENC	55	Bibliography
54	Aging	90	Biography Info—BH
47	Airline Info—AT	65	Book Marketing Ideas
46	Airline Info—BH	44	Book Publishing Ideas
112	Airline Info—General	14	Brochure Development
27	Allied Van Lines	41	Business Growth Magazine
105	ARMA	96	Business Leader
85	Article Ideas—Business	1	Business Plans
127	Article Ideas—Personal	172	Call Home American
84	Article Markets	48	Car Rental Info
25	Articles BH 99-2002	88	Carlson Learning
22	Artwork—Printing Info	20	Certificate—BH
16	ASAE	167	Checkbook Organizer
165	ASJA	142	Clients 2000
76	Association Executives of NC	178	Clients 2001
12	Audio and Video, TV Production	114	Clients 2002
187	Avery Label Pro	5	Computer Backup and
37	Back of Room Sales		Maintenance

However you choose to organize your files, remember that a filing system is only as good as the index that describes it. A File Index is a living and changing document; it must evolve just like the organization that creates it. So, use it regularly and update it whenever you add or delete a file. These tips will help:

Keep the File Index as simple as possible. For example, "Airlines" (alphabetical by company) is preferable to listing each airline name. This also means that your index will not become outdated whenever you add or remove an airline.

Keep the index as short as possible. Single-space your File Index. In the margins you can handwrite the file titles you wish to add to the system. If the file titles are short enough, you may want to put two columns on a page.

Keep copies of the index handy. Chances are the File Index will be too long to post on the front of the first cabinet. Instead, one copy should be in the front of the file cabinet itself, filed in a separate folder labeled "File Index" and highlighted in a bright color for easy visibility, and another copy at the desk of each person who uses the file system. If your office has a large file system with many file cabinets, create a filing-system manual to keep on top of the filing cabinet for ready reference (see Chapter 18). When I travel, I carry the File Index with me so I can note where papers need to be filed as I collect them.

Periodically update and refine the File Index on your computer. Check all the users' copies of the index and see what files were added or deleted. Enter the changes in the original computer file, making sure to include the date of revision so that users can quickly identify whether the File Index is recent. Print out new copies for all locations.

CHAPTER 5

Manage Your Contact Information

Are adhesive notes, business cards, message slips and various other scraps of paper littered across your desk and jammed into the drawers? You can't part with them, because each has a phone number, address or other miscellaneous—but important—piece of contact information that you want to keep. Does your e-mail box suffer from the same syndrome?

Perhaps you've got a dog-eared card file or a contact-manager program on your computer that no longer meets your needs, or a system inherited from your predecessor that never worked for you in the first place. The simplest—and often the most effective—solution is to just start over and create a new contact filing system.

Whichever tool you choose, the method for starting over is the same as for starting a new filing system. Add new names and addresses as you get them and pick up and refile entries from the old system as needed. Keep your old system nearby or online until you've exhausted its useful information and then throw it away or delete it, or just set it aside if you're afraid to throw it away.

The next time you get a business card, a message slip, or an e-mail message with a phone number that you want to keep, ask yourself, "If I want to contact this person again, what word will I think of first?" The answer is a key word. It may be the person's last name (although you may want to use the first names of family and friends), the name of the company, the service they provide, or even the name of whoever introduced you or where you met.

Many of my clients still find a card file to be a valuable organizing tool— regardless of what other electronic or non-electronic system they use.

In many electronic systems, how you identify the entry won't affect your ability to retrieve it, because you can search the entire database by whatever word you choose. In addition, you can enter in more data altogether, and the more you enter, the more ways you will have to find the names and numbers you need.

Choose Your Weapon

Your first decision will be where to store the information. Before the days of computers, most people used a card file. Now many people use contact-manager programs on their computers or personal digital assistants exclusively. Some use one of each, for different purposes, in a combination strategy.

The Old Standard—A Card File

Why choose a paper system over an electronic one? Some people just feel more comfortable with paper than with a computer screen, although a growing number of people recognize and appreciate the increased capabilities of an electronic system.

One big advantage of a traditional card file is that it allows you to file business cards as soon as you receive them, without having to transcribe the information elsewhere. Use 3 x 5-inch cards so that you can staple or tape business cards right onto them. Rolodex® is the most common brand of such cards, but Bates, Eldon and Rubbermaid also make them.

Even people who use a contact-manager program or a personal digital assistant (PDA) find a traditional card file to be of great value. In my own case, I keep information in my card file that I want to retrieve quickly, even though it might duplicate information I keep in my computer, such as the names and numbers of clients or colleagues with whom I often speak.

As a professional organizer, I find that many of my clients still find a card file to be a valuable organizing tool—no matter what other electronic or non-electronic system they use.

Computer Databases, Including Contact-Manager Programs

A database program allows you to enter whatever kind of information you want—name, title, address, phone, fax, who introduced you, client history, and so on—and to search, sort, and retrieve the information by whichever criteria you choose.

Contact-manager programs, such as *Act!* (www.act.com), *Maximizer* (www.maximizer.com), and *Telemagic* (www.telemagic.com), go a step further by combining database, calendar, and word-processing capabilities. For example, when I'm going on a business trip to Arizona, I can use my computer's contact-manager program to retrieve every contact I have in that state, as well as print out mailing labels for them. While I'm in Arizona, if I speak with a prospective client who says, "Please give me a call next June," I can enter a reminder in my contact-manager program for June 1. That day the program will automatically present me with a reminder—announced with the sound of a bell or without, depending on my preference. The word-processor feature provides a variety of form letters that make it easy for me to write letters to my contacts in Arizona and record what I have sent.

The key-word concept also applies to a contact-manager program. Many of these systems allow you to enter information by primary and secondary source. For example, if a meeting planner requests information from me for a prospective speaking engagement, I use the name of the association for the primary source, and the meeting planner's name as the secondary. I'm more apt to recall the name of the association if I'm looking up the information, but if the meeting planner calls me, I can retrieve what I need by his or her name.

Personal Digital Assistants

Personal digital assistants have been referred to by various names, including portable electronic organizers and personal information managers, but most people nowadays call them personal digital assistants, or PDAs. This

Contact-manager programs combine database, calendar, and word-processing capabilities.

TIP: A BUSINESS-CARD SHORTCUT

A business-card scanner is a small device that can read the information from a business card and place it in a contact-manager program or export it directly to your e-mail software. The price of scanners ranges from $50 to a few hundred dollars, depending on the type and features. If you have to enter all your contact information yourself and you have a pile of cards waiting for entry, such a device might be worth the cost.

tool lets you take your names and numbers—and in many instances, your calendar—with you in compact form. They range from the size of a watch to a small pocketbook. The simplest model stores about 100 names, while the most advanced stores thousands of names and allows you to create and fax documents, access the Web, send and receive e-mail and, with transfer software, send and receive files to and from your PC.

Depending on the amount of memory and the bells and whistles, PDAs range in price from under $100 to $1,000. You may have to pay more for transfer software to send and receive files from your PC.

A variety of circumstances—some explainable, some not—can cause any electronic device to fail. You must have a backup system, such as a paper printout or an electronic backup on a computer; it's insurance you can't live without.

My Combination Strategy

I use a combination of tools to maintain and give me access to my professional and personal contacts:

- **My contact-manager program contains information about current,** past, and prospective clients. I use it to keep track of services I have provided to them, as well as marketing efforts I've made with them. This program is loaded on my laptop computer for access when I'm traveling, and when I am in the office, the laptop plugs into our office network for easy updating.

When I am on the road, we use e-mail to update the contact information in *Act!* (described above).

- **My card file at my office contains the names of services that I use,** such as computer repair, graphics, airlines, and so on; clients with whom I speak frequently; and colleagues and family members with whom I speak when I'm in the office.
- **A small leather telephone book,** which I carry in my briefcase, contains the personal and professional numbers that I most frequently use.

This system has developed over time and still works for me, although the time may come when I will purchase a PDA so that, when I travel, I can have quicker access to more contact information without having to boot up my laptop.

There are probably dozens of possibilities for managing your contact information. Some of my clients put all their information on personal digital assistants, others in their laptop computers, and still others rely completely on manual systems.

Remember, as with paper, the important questions are: Does it work? Do I like it? As your work changes, so may your answers.

CHAPTER 6

Make the Most of Your Calendar

I have found that, for most people, 40% of the paper they receive gets tossed in the wastebasket, 40% goes in the file cabinet, and the remaining 20% requires action. How they handle that last 20% has a significant impact on their productivity. The same observation applies to the information they receive by computer.

Frequently we shuffle papers from one side of the desk to the other or allow e-mail to linger in our e-mail in-boxes because when we look at the item, it reminds us of several things we need to do. We feel overwhelmed, and we put it aside. Here's a two-part strategy you can use to eliminate that habit:

- **First,** when you identify something that requires action, ask: Am I the appropriate person to act on this, or should I delegate it to someone else—before it's too late, and I feel guilty about dumping it on him or her?
- **Second,** ask: Is there a deadline on this piece of paper? If not, good time management may dictate that you create a deadline.

With a due date established, you are ready to act or pass the information on to whomever you have assigned the task, and you are ready to use one of the most important organizing tools in your life—your calendar, the focus of this chapter.

Smart Use of Your Calendar

You can eliminate a surprising amount of paper and computer files by using your calendar. The key is to

If a meeting notice contains more essential information than will fit in your calendar, put it into your pending file for future reference.

extract the information you need from the paper or the document, enter it in your calendar, and then use the wastebasket. Many people I know use their calendar as a filing cabinet, stuffing papers inside the front and back covers and in between pages. That takes lots of precious space in a briefcase, makes it harder to use your calendar and to find things, and means you risk dropping and losing stuff every time you use the calendar, to say nothing of looking less than professional.

Here are some of the ways that you can eliminate clutter by using your calendar.

Meeting Notices

Let's say you receive a meeting notice in your in-box or in your e-mail. You can enter the information—time, place, telephone number and e-mail address for additional information—directly into your calendar. If there's more essential information on the notice (such as an agenda and directions) than will fit in your calendar, you can note the name of the meeting in your calendar and put the notice itself into your Pending File for future reference (see Chapter 8 for more information on various kind of Action Files).

Be careful not to put so much information into your calendar that it becomes unreadable.

Future or Conflicting Events

Suppose you read in a newsletter about a seminar that you would like to attend. If you leave the notice on your desk so that you won't forget about the seminar, you are likely to handle that document dozens of times. But if it doesn't resurface on the appropriate day, you have accomplished nothing. Instead, mark the seminar on your calendar—in pencil—both on the day you need to make your reservation and on the day of the event. If you find that you have slotted more than one activity for the same time, you can deliberately choose how you will spend your time, instead of reacting to whichever notice happens to wend its way to the top of the pile of stuff.

Follow-Up

If you've written a letter and you need a reply in two weeks, make a note in your calendar on the due date, "Heard from John?" This way, you use your calendar not only for appointments, but also for effective follow-up. If there are specific materials that you want to check when you follow-up, note in your calendar where they are, for example, "See XYZ file."

Appointments With Ourselves

Many of us are great about using our calendar to make appointments with others, but rarely make appointments with ourselves. That's unfortunate, because the people I've found who are most successful in managing their time and reaching their goals are those who make appointments with themselves to complete specific tasks and check on specific issues.

Let's say that you attend a meeting and agree to complete a certain task. Instead of writing a note on the legal pad you've brought along and hoping it will resurface when you need to remember, make a quick calculation about when you need to begin work on that task and mark it on your calendar. You avoid creating additional pieces of paper that you must track, and you'll be reminded of what you need to do at exactly the right time (see also Chapter 8).

If there's something specific you want to do for yourself—like clean out your file drawer or spend time on your to-read pile (see page 80), make an appointment with yourself, just as you would with someone else.

Some people hesitate to use this approach because they're afraid of becoming compulsive. They shudder at the thought of, say, conversing with a colleague and abruptly saying, "I need to go now. It's time for me to catch up on my reading!" I am *not* suggesting that you become inflexible. But using your calendar as a time-management tool will help you be realistic about your time. If you've blocked out an hour to write the report from your last committee meeting and decide something else is a higher priority, you can choose another time to write the report.

The people I've found who are most successful in managing their time and reaching their goals are those who make appointments with themselves.

Does your calendar work? Do you like it? If the answer to either question is no, begin now to find a replacement.

Choose Your Calendar or Planner

I've never met anyone who was comfortable with the way they managed their paper and their time who didn't also have a calendar or planner they counted on. Choosing from the dozens of calendars and planners on the market can be overwhelming, let alone learning to use one. But doing so is a major step toward gaining control of your work and personal life and should be very high on your priority list.

When evaluating your calendar, ask those now-familiar questions: Does it work? Do I like it? If the answer to either question is no, begin now to find a replacement. You'll probably use it 300 days out of the year, and it can be a big investment.

Some companies require, or at least strongly encourage, employees to use a particular product. Over the years I've seen many dusty planning books laying on shelves because they simply didn't work for their owners. A better approach is to gather ideas from the people around you whom you admire. But be realistic: Don't assume that because a product is perfect for them it will be perfect for you. Ask them what they like and don't like about their system, and determine which of those things matter to you.

I've never met anyone who didn't have at least one complaint about their calendar: It's too big to fit easily on a desk or in a purse, briefcase or shirt pocket; it's too little and doesn't have enough writing space; or even, it doesn't come in the right color. As with many other things in life, there are trade-offs.

Choose the calendar or planner that meets the greatest number of your needs, and adapt it. The discussion that follows will help you make the big decisions about choosing a calendar or planner.

Daily, Weekly, Monthly or More?

The first decision you need to make when picking a calendar is how much of your schedule you want to see at one time—a day, a week, a month, a year, or a combination. (I prefer a combination, which I describe below.) Time-management experts say that scheduling time in weekly blocks is the most effective way to be proactive with your life rather than reactive. My personal experience supports that assertion.

For years I used a daily calendar that had the advantage of providing lots of writing space. I selected one in which I could schedule the day's fixed appointments on the left-hand side of the page and write my to-do list on the right-hand side, including phone calls to make, follow-up actions, and so on. The front of the calendar provided a monthly calendar where I noted nonnegotiable appointments around which I manipulated the rest of my schedule—business travel, major events, important family commitments, and so on.

However, in recent years I've found that I must make more choices about what I will and won't do. A calendar with a weekly format works better for me now because I can track how I am meeting my priorities. Say, for example, my goal is to exercise three times a week—something many of us want to accomplish during the workday, but have difficulty getting around to. I make appointments with myself—and check them off when I get them done. If I get to midweek and there are no checks by my exercise appointments, I know I have to get moving.

Paper or Electronic?

Another decision you need to make is whether to use a paper calendar, a portable electronic organizer with calendar features, or a computer program for your desktop or laptop computer.

I know people who've never successfully used a paper calendar who find a computer-based program indispensable. Like paper calendars, these come packaged in various ways—for instance, as a feature of a word-processing package, as a separate, add-on software program, or as a pre-installed feature on a hand-held device.

One big advantage of an electronic calendar is the ability to search for information in a variety of ways. For

> One big advantage of an electronic calendar is the ability to search for information in a variety of ways.

FROM MY FILES: ADAPTING A CALENDAR

Shortly after Christmas a few years ago, I was sitting on an airplane next to a woman who was browsing through a beautiful red leather planner. She sighed audibly, and I asked her what was wrong. "Oh," she replied, "I must be hopeless. My husband gave me this beautiful calendar for Christmas to help me get organized, and I don't even know how to use it!" We spent the next two hours discussing how she could adapt it to meet her needs, and when we parted at the baggage claim she asked, "Did my husband arrange for you, too?"

You can adapt your calendar to your needs, as well. If you're lugging around a big calendar, for example, but you like lots of writing space, use adhesive notes to write reminders and stick them to the appropriate calendar pages. When you've completed the task, throw the note away. For example, I use a 3 x 5-inch note for keeping a list of miscellaneous items that I need to purchase. That way, when I'm running errands and pass a store that carries a particular item, I can avoid making a special trip.

Perhaps you have found a terrific weekly calendar, but you also need to look at the entire month. Add a peel-off pocket to the front or back of the weekly calendar, and put a small monthly calendar in the pocket.

example, if you want to find every instance of contact that you've had with a particular client, you can search by the client name and get all the information you need within seconds. These programs allow you to print out hard copies of your calendar, and it's easy to make backup copies for protection. If your computer is networked with the person who schedules your appointments, it's simple to share information without transcribing data from one calendar to another. Some calendar programs have time-management features, including a to-do list and tickler (reminder) function. One client selected a computer-based calendar because he had difficulty reading his own handwriting.

On the other hand, many people who had used paper versions successfully, but felt compelled to try the latest technology, missed the paper. I fall into that category. I feel a sense of security in being able to hold my schedule, and knowing I can always access it, without depending on technology.

Calendar or Planner?

Many companies have begun calling their calendar products "planners" because they contain more tools and information than just a calendar. These include project planners, logs for telephone calls, forms for recording meeting minutes, or even geographical or overseas travel information. There are even planners that double as purses and briefcases.

You can spend $15 or more than $200 on elaborate planning components, but an expensive one won't necessarily work better than a lower-priced one. Keep in mind that you don't have to use every tool that a particular planning product includes. Choose the tools that work for you, and omit or ignore the others.

If you want more than a calendar, but can't find a planner that meets your needs, design your own. It's as simple as taking a three-ring binder and adding subject dividers. You can create your own forms, or use pre-designed ones from various companies to suit your needs. Cost doesn't necessarily correlate with quality or effectiveness.

More Than One Calendar?

If your business life is basically nine-to-five, then you'll need a calendar at the office. You will also need a calendar for your personal life, and you might need to take it with you to the office, since most people end up doing personal business sometime during the workday. But chances are your business and personal life overlap, as is true for me, and you don't want to run the risk of not having one of your calendars with you when you need it. If that's the case, then your best option is a master calendar that reflects both areas of your life and that you carry with you virtually all the time. For example, my hair stylist is in high demand, and I need to schedule her weeks in advance. I take my master calendar with me to each appointment so I can schedule my next one while I'm there, thus avoiding an extra telephone call.

In addition to your master calendar (and other satellite calendars), you may have calendars for specific func-

The cost of a calendar or planner doesn't necessarily correlate with quality or effectiveness.

TOOL: BARBARA HEMPHILL'S CALENDAR

Here's a sample of my paper calendar. I use the yearly section for an overview of what lies ahead (last six months shown below). Abbreviations and short descriptions let me know:

- Where I'll be (Boston on the 7th, for example)
- Family schedules (I use a different color pencil for each family member)
- Important events (Pat H. birthday on 4th)

	YEARLY PLANNER					
SUNDAY	**MONDAY**	**TUESDAY**	**WEDNESDAY**	**THURSDAY**	**FRIDAY**	**SATURDAY**
					1 *CANADA DAY*	2
3	4 PAT H. *INDEPENDENCE DAY*	5	6	7 ADIE/CHUCK BOSTON	8	9
10	11	12 Ron-MARIE	13	14 BETTY	15	16
17	18	19 ABERNATHY	20	21	22 PAM	23
24	25 BOOK FAIR	26	27	28	29	30 BOBBIE
31	1	2 WINSTON-SALEM	3	4 — ASHEVILLE	5	6 NAPO BOARD
7	8	9 — VACATION —	10	11	12	13
14 JOLLA-21	15	16 — VACATION —	17	18	19	20
21	22 — ATLANTA —	23	24	25	26	27 DUKE
28	29 HAIRCUT	30	31	1	2	3
4	5 *ABOF OA*	6 *ROSH HASHANAH*	7 HEIDI TO SCHOOL	8	9 CSA	10 AT/DRILL
11 AT/DRILL	12 DUKE	13 AT/BH ANNIVERSARY	14	15 *YOM KIPPUR*	16	17
18	19	20	21 NATION'S BANK NCSU	22 ASJA — ASHEVILLE —	23	24
25	26	27 HOWARD COUNTY	28	29 WASH DC	30	1
2	3 RADIO TOUR —	4 — GET ORGANIZED WEEK —	5	6	7	8
9	10 CHARLOTTE *COLUMBUS DAY* *THANKSGIVING DAY (CAN)*	11	12 *COLUMBUS DAY*	13 BEN - 21 HEIDI —	14	15 STANTON
16	17 — NAPO	18	19	20 NCSU	21	22
23	24	25	26	27	28	29
30	31 *HALLOWEEN*	1 *ELECTION DAY*	2	3	4 — NAPO RETREAT —	5
6	7	8	9 ASTD	10	11 *VETERAN'S DAY*	12
13	14	15 WASH DC	16	17	18	19
20	21 NAPO - DC	22	23 HEIDI	24 *THANKSGIVING DAY*	25	26
27	28 *CHANUKAH BEGINS*	29	30	1	2	3
4	5 — FT. LAUDERDALE —	6	7	8	9	10
11	13	13	14	15	16	17
18	19	20	21 HEIDI —	22	23	24
25 *CHRISTMAS DAY*	26	27	28	29	30	31

Month labels (left column): JUL, AUG, SEP, OCT, NOV, DEC

Appointments, daily to-do's, and projects go in the weekly section—on the left-hand page shown below—under my different roles. Expense notations are on the right-hand page that is not shown here.

PLANNING FOR THE WEEK OF: *AUGUST 22*

WEEKLY LISTS OF ACTIVITIES BY CATEGORIES

H & A	SPEAKER/WRITER	NAPO	FAMILY
TRIANGLE AD	HEARD FROM TIME ? (CE)	CALL CHRIS (C)	CHAIRS / BED TO
NCSU	NCSU SEMINAR PLAN	LETTER TO ARIZ	CHURCH 878-9335
BROCHURE COPY	TAMING CORRECTIONS	BY-LAW REVISION	HEARD FROM MARGARET ?
VIDEO FEEDBACK ?		CONTRACT	MORTGAGE APPLICATION
FLYERS RE DUKE		NEW ADDRESS	CALL LANDSCAPER

RSVP - SK WEDDING (P)

DAILY THINGS-TO-DO

MONDAY 22	TUESDAY 23	WEDNESDAY 24	THURSDAY 25
TAMING CORRECTIONS	MARY HIGGINS	CALL RENETTE	CALL CHICAGO (P)
BOB BAILEY	924-5267	834-3722 (W)	
700-902-8202	ALEX - GOING TONIGHT?	CHRISTY - NAPO ? (CE)	
MOLLY GLANDER	JAN SWANSON	600-322-9753	
CALL RON FALKIN	800-790-1342		
REMAX 242-3100	INFO TO STAPLES		
CALL GREER —			
SEE 8/11			
CALL SUSANNE			

APPOINTMENTS

7 DADDY'S BIRTHDAY	7	7	7 BREAKFAST / CLUB - K.C.
8	8	8	8
9	9 NATION'S BANK	9	9 NCSU - DELIVER ART
10	10 ROD - 829-6633	10	10
11	11	11	11
12	12	12	12 MOLLY / KAY
1	1	1	1 RE COVEY
2 HAIRCUT	2	2	2
3	3:30 NCSU - PAM SMITH	3	3
4	4 2190 BERLIN Rd.	4	4
5	5 501-3470	5	5
6	6	6	6
7	7	7	7
8	8 ENNIS	8	8
9	9	9	9

WRITING (Monday 3-6)

SUCCESS SEMINAR GREENSBORO HILTON (Wednesday)

PLANNER PAD®

P=Pending **LM**=Left message **CE**=Calls expected **D**=Discuss **C**=Call

tions. For example, a calendar on my office wall indicates my travel schedule so colleagues know when I'll be available. Many offices use a huge wall calendar to schedule projects with intermediate deadlines. One caution: If you put it up, use it consistently, or you risk people not taking deadlines seriously.

Combine Your Phone Book With Your Calendar?

Everyone I know carries at least some phone numbers and addresses at all times. In a loose-leaf planner, you can carry the same telephone section forward from year to year, while in bound ones, you have to recopy that section each year. Manufacturers of the latter style contend that it's a good practice to annually purge numbers you carry with you. That's probably good advice, but many people would never do it. I've frequently had clients who carry two years' calendars because they didn't have time to recopy the phone numbers and addresses from one year's calendar to the next. Although the planner I use has a section for phone numbers, I carry and use a separate phone book—a small leather book that fits in any purse I carry. It even works for social occasions, when I won't carry my planner but may still be networking and want to make notations of people I meet.

How My Calendar Reflects My Roles in Life

Choosing your calendar is a personal decision. The main thing is to choose it and use it—consistently.

I personally use the Executive Planner Pad (www.plannerpads.com), which measures 8½ x 11 inches and is about a half-inch thick (see the sample on the preceding pages or at www.plannerpads.com). It allows me to combine my calendar and my to-do lists (discussed in the next chapter) into one book that's small enough to easily carry in my briefcase.

TIP: SAFEKEEPING FOR YOUR CALENDAR

Whichever type of calendar you choose, I encourage you to do whatever you can to minimize losing it. If it's electronic—on your computer or in an electronic organizer—back it up, as you would any other computer file. If it's paper, put a note in the front saying "Return for Reward" with contact information that you feel is safe to provide, probably your work address and phone number.

My calendar provides two pages for each week. The pages are divided into thirds horizontally. The bottom third is for noting fixed appointments. The middle third is for noting the things I want to accomplish during the day, such as phone calls to make, letters to write, and so on. I can use the top third to list current major projects with notes about what I need to accomplish that week.

So that I can work on the issue of balance in my life, I have found it helpful to use the top third of each page to identify the major roles in my life and what I expect to accomplish that week, based on the principles of Stephen Covey's *First Things First* (see pages 72–83). For example, my current major roles include business owner, communicator (writing, speaking), National Association of Professional Organizers member; National Speakers Association member, wife and household manager, family member, and friend and neighbor. At the end of each week, I look at all my roles, and determine what I hope to accomplish in each of these roles during the week. Some roles may have no goals in a specific week. For example, "friend and neighbor" may be blank if I am going out of town on business. (See Chapters 7 and 8 for more on coordinating your calendar with your to-do list and your Action Files.)

CHAPTER 7

Eliminate Clutter With Your To-Do List

Desks are often cluttered with pieces of paper we keep as reminders of things we want to do—review the insurance coverage, update the marketing plan, or revise the company policy manual. In my experience, these items break down into two major categories: those representing things you want to be done at a specific time, such as sending out an agenda for a meeting, and those you want to do sometime in the future, such as cleaning out your filing cabinet. To eliminate this clutter, first block out time on your calendar to complete the to-do's in the first category and file any needed information in your Action Files (see Chapter 8). This will also provide a more realistic picture of where your time is going and help you manage it more effectively. Then make a to-do list of the second category—projects you want to do someday, but for which you haven't identified a specific time—and file away any papers you need to keep until you are actually ready to take action.

For example, say I get a catalog in the mail that has information about a product that I am thinking about buying. Instead of cluttering up my desk with the catalog, I can make an entry on my to-do list that says, "Purchase new widget." I can then file the catalog with my other catalogs (with a page number of the widget noted on the front) or file it under "Shopping Information" or "Widget." If you are afraid that you will forget where you filed the catalog, make a note on your to-do lists that says "See catalog in [name of file]."

To Do or Not to Do—That Is the Question!

Perhaps the toughest part of organizing is deciding what to do and what not to do. In the book *First Things First*, author Stephen Covey, with Roger and Rebecca Merrill (Fireside), suggests that how we spend time can be divided into four quadrants:

- **Quadrant I: Urgent and Important**
- **Quadrant II: Important but not Urgent**
- **Quadrant III: Urgent but not Important**
- **Quadrant IV: Not Urgent and not Important**

The status of "Urgent" is usually determined by an outside influence, such as a deadline imposed by your boss, while "Important" is determined by our values—what really matters to us and what we want to accomplish at work and home. The latter might include such goals as completing a project on time and with high quality, hiring a new assistant, getting a new job, spending more time with your family, and taking better care of your body.

For example:

- **Quadrant I** could be "It's April 13 and I haven't done anything about my taxes."
- **Quadrant II** could be exercise. However, if you don't exercise, but your doctor tells you to lose 20 pounds or risk a heart attack, it becomes a Quadrant I.
- **Quadrant III** could be a telephone call from a sales representative while you were working on your monthly analysis report.
- **Quadrant IV** could be that lunch you didn't really want to have with the person to whom you didn't have the guts to say no.

I attended one of Stephen Covey's seminars, and he asked his listeners to "name one thing that, if you did it consistently, would improve the quality of your life." Try it yourself. If you're like most people, your answer (whatever it is) falls into Quadrant II, Important but not Urgent.

I learned that I had eliminated most of Quadrants III and IV from my to-do list, except when I was procrastinating—for example, cleaning off my desk when I had planned to look for some new sources for clients. But to my horror, I discovered that I virtually lived in Quadrant I. Everything I was doing was not only important to me, but urgent, too, because I was trying to do too much and I was always on deadline.

What's the answer? I'm still learning, but here are some things I am sure of:

- **Deciding** whether to do or not to do something requires continually checking your to-do list with your mission statement (see page 12 of Chapter 1).
- **The more I do,** the less I enjoy.
- **Just because** I choose not to do something now doesn't mean I can't do it later.
- **Sometimes** I can get satisfaction by doing something less than perfectly.

I can choose to do a Quadrant II activity today, such as spending time with my daughter who will be leaving in two days, consequently putting myself in Quadrant I with work tomorrow—but that is my choice.

Where Should You Keep Your To-Do List?

Your to-do list can be located in various places—a section of your calendar (as I mentioned in describing my daily planner), a personal digital assistant, a computer file, a separate notebook or pad, or even a wall chart or whiteboard (with erasable markers). As with other systems I've described, consistency is crucial, so develop a system that will be easy for you to use. If your system is not portable, make sure that you have a method, such as notecards carried in your pocket or briefcase, for recording the ideas that occur to you when you are not in your office. When you return to your office, you can incorporate them into your system.

> Deciding whether to do or not to do something requires continually checking your to-do list with your mission statement.

73

Organize Your To-Do List

One basic principle when organizing anything is to put like items together. This technique will work for your to-do lists, as well. I've found it helpful to categorize my to-do's by my roles, as I described previously in the section on calendars. Other favorite categories of mine are errands, books, and Web sites to check. Consequently, I minimize trips around the city to run errands, I have a list of books that I want to see whenever I go to the library or bookstore, and I spend an evening once a month on the computer checking out Web sites that interest me.

Look at Your Accomplishments

A friend of mine says that he makes lists of things he's already done because it's fun to check them off. If you constantly make to-do lists that you don't complete, try the exercise of making a list of what you did accomplish. What quadrants were they in? Identify those things that you could have:

- **Eliminated from your list:** Did you do them to avoid doing something else?
- **Delegated:** Were you the most appropriate person to do those tasks?
- **Delayed:** Could you have waited until a more appropriate time to do them?
- **Simplified:** Could you have written a quick e-mail message instead of a formal letter?

CHAPTER 8

Take Action

So let's review: We've discussed how clutter is postponed decisions. As you go through your in-box or sort the papers on your desk or in your office, you can eliminate much of it by applying the Art of Wastebasketry (see pages 19–25) and even more by using your calendar, to-do list, card file, or computer database program, and your Reference Files. But you will still face papers that require your action.

If you don't have much left on your desk after tossing and filing, you may be quite comfortable with just one to-do file or pile, if you prefer—or maybe three of them, prioritized by urgency. However, many of my clients and I find that that is simply not enough given the many hats we wear and the workloads we bear.

You can sort the remaining paper in a variety of ways. One would be to sort them by project or activity, such as a trip or a meeting. But how can you sort many individual and miscellaneous papers—unrelated to a larger project—that require action, such as making a phone call to inquire about a new product or writing a letter to thank a colleague for referring a new client?

I find it helpful to separate my Action Files into two types: temporary action and permanent action:

- **Temporary Action Files** are for things that you need to do infrequently, such as write a report or plan a meeting, and generally involve several pieces of paper. These files have a name (such as project, trip, or event) and can be filed alphabetically (or numerically into the action location if you use *Taming the Paper Tiger* software).

As the volume of paper on your desk increases, your ability to find the paper when you need it will decrease. You will be more likely to find it if you put it in an Action File.

■ **Permanent Action Files** are for keeping track of paper relating to actions that you take recurrently. To decide what permanent Action Files you need, ask yourself: What is the next action I need to take on this piece of paper? The word *next* is crucial: The paper may remind you to do a dozen things, but you can do only one at a time. Typical answers are to call, write, or read. You can create a permanent Action File for each category.

Define Your Next Action in the Real World

It frequently takes some thinking to figure out your next action. For example, say that you receive a memo from Terry with questions about a contract. You might initially respond, "I have to call Terry," but then you realize that you first need to review the contract, then discuss it with Susan, who's out of the office until Friday. If she has an assistant or you have access to her calendar, your first action would be to make an appointment with Susan. If neither is so, you would leave a voice- or e-mail message that you need to talk with her, or you would make a note in your calendar to call her on Friday. Then you would put the contract in your Permanent Action File for Review or Read.

Out of Sight, Out of Mind?

"All well and good," you say, "but if I put a piece of paper in a file, I'd never see it or do anything with it." If you have fewer than 20 pieces of paper on your desk, the system for Action Files that I'm proposing may not be necessary. But as the volume of paper on your desk increases, your ability to find the paper when you need it will decrease, and you will be more likely to find it if you put it in an Action File.

You may wonder, "How will I remember to look in those files?" You don't have to remember. Your calendar notations will remind you to look in the appropriate file at the appropriate time. Simply mark a symbol on your calendar (as the following section of text will describe) to remind you to look. Papers in your call file will automatically remind you of calls to make—and possibly prompt you to make others.

Suggested Action Categories

In this section, I'll describe categories of action. One advantage of gathering together similar actions by category is that you can increase your productivity. For instance, if you're making one phone call, you can probably make another one in just a few more minutes—if you don't have to spend time looking for the paper you need to make the additional call. Another major advantage is that your Action Files will be a good place to start if you have the opportunity to delegate work to other people; you will have essentially divided your job into categories of action.

Don't be intimidated by the how numerous the categories are; you won't need them all, and you may find that you need others that aren't described.

As you read through the list, if the whole idea of creating Action Files seems overwhelming, choose a few categories that particularly appeal to you and try just those. Call, Write or Read might be just enough to start with. A file labeled "Calls Expected," described below, has been a favorite of my clients through the years; the problem of finding a piece of paper that you need to discuss with a return caller seems to be a common one.

Calendar Entry
If you use an electronic calendar, you may want to put all the papers that require calendar notes into one Action File so that you can enter them all at once.

Call
Many times a telephone call is the next action required in response to a piece of paper. In addition to putting the paper in your call file, you may want to make a note on your calendar on the day that you need to make the

Your calendar notations will remind you to look in the appropriate file at the appropriate time.

call. Noting a "C" next to the calendar entry will remind you that the paper you need to make is in the Call file.

Calls Expected

How many times have you experienced this scenario? You phone someone who isn't in, so you leave a message in the person's voice mail and put the piece of paper on your desk. Then days or even weeks later, you get a call that begins, "This is Jerry returning your call." You get a knot in your stomach as you frantically try to remember why you called him—or even who he is.

If you have placed the paper in your Calls Expected file, you won't risk embarrassment or have to make another call because you couldn't find what you needed.

If you need to hear from that person by a specific date or time, put a note in your calendar or that day's to-do list, "Heard from Jerry?" with a "CE" noted by that entry to remind you where you put the paper in question.

If you were simply returning a call and the ball is now in the other person's court, leave the relevant paper in the Calls Expected file for awhile. On the paper, note the date that you returned the call, so that you will know how long it has been since you called. If you receive no response within an appropriate length of time, toss the piece of paper.

Data Entry

Some of the papers in your in-box or floating on your desk contain information that needs to be entered into your computer. It's more efficient to make several entries at the same time—or to delegate the task to someone else. When you've entered the material from this file into the computer, you can throw out the papers, pass them on to the next person who needs them, or, if you must save them, file them in the appropriate Reference File.

You may be wondering, Why, if I'm helping you tame your paper tiger, would I suggest that you keep any paper after you've entered the information in your computer? Because sometimes you need to keep the paper, say, for tax purposes. But before you stow it away, always ask first: What's the worst possible thing that would happen if I didn't have this piece of paper? If you can live with the possibilities, toss it.

Discuss

We often can't act on a matter until we've discussed it with someone else, and we all have certain people with whom we routinely discuss issues. The Discuss category will contain several files labeled with those persons' names and filed alphabetically by first name or title, such as Accountant. In this category, I like to use colored files, assigning one color to each person with whom I regularly speak, so that I can recognize the appropriate file quickly when someone steps into my office or I get a phone call.

Errands

Many of our to-do's—such as getting a document notarized, visiting a new office-supply store, or checking out a resource at the library—must be done outside the office. If you traditionally have dozens of errands, you could organize them into subcategories by location, deadlines for completion, or type of errand (for example, office-supply store or pharmacy).

Expense Reimbursement

If you incur expenses that your employer will reimburse, you can keep your receipts here for easy retrieval when you are ready to submit an expense report.

If you have dozens of errands, you could organize them into subcategories by location, deadlines for completion, or type of errand (for example, office supply store or pharmacy).

TIP: MANAGE YOUR TO-READ PILE

Overwhelmed by the piles of reports, magazines, journals, and newsletters sitting around your office? Consider these tips:

- **Accept** that you will probably never be able to read everything you would like to—or think you should.
- **Read with a pen in your hand.** On the front cover of the publication, note the page number and subject of articles that particularly interest you, so that you can find them quickly.
- **Check the table of contents** in a magazine when it first comes in. Tear out and staple together the articles you want to read. Put them in a file folder in your briefcase to read when you are waiting for an appointment or riding the subway.

- **Avoid a perfectionistic approach.** Instead of putting aside that newsletter until you can read it perfectly, and then discovering that you're reading the information too late for it to be of value, scan it for timely information when it first arrives.
- **Delegate your reading.** If you have support staff, train them to scan publications for items that might be of interest to you and highlight them.
- **Create a separate filing system** for articles you want to read. You'll find them much more quickly there than in a pile of magazines behind your desk. Your motivation to read the articles and your ability to determine their value will be much greater if they relate to a current problem.

Online

This is a place to put a list of Web sites that you want to check or papers that you want to handle with e-mail. It's also useful if you use mail-order catalogs frequently or you're responsible for ordering office supplies or equipment.

Pay

This file is for bills to pay. Because I have a home office, I pay both my personal and business bills from there, and I divide my bills accordingly into three categories: business, personal (which I pay monthly), and donations (which I consider separately once each quarter).

Pending

This category is for papers that you'll need at a specific date in the future. (It can also be called by other names, such as Bring-Up or Tickler.) For example, if you sign up for a seminar and receive your tickets with a map and directions, put the information in your Pending File and note a "P" in your calendar on the day you will need it, next to the seminar entry.

Remember, that's "P" for pending, not for procrastinating. When you're tempted to put something here because you're not sure what to do with it, ask yourself: What am I going to know tomorrow that I don't know today? If your answer is "nothing," you need to look further into the issue to find out what other category of Action File the paper truly belongs in.

You can create Pending Files in three ways, one of which may best suit your needs:

- **31 daily files,** as well as additional files for upcoming months. If you use this system, you won't need to note in your calendar the date when you'll need something, but you will need to check each day's Pending File. When I tried this approach, I found I wasn't consistent about that, and, of course, when I was traveling, I wasn't in my office to check the file anyway.
- **12 monthly files** and one for the next year. This is the system I use. I check the file at the beginning of each month or at the end of the previous month. All the items in the Pending File that have to be retrieved on a particular day are noted in my calendar with a "P."
- **A single file** with items arranged chronologically. This is appropriate only if you don't have many pending issues. Be sure to put a note in your calendar to remind you to retrieve the paper you need.

Photocopy

Often, you can't take the next action on something until you make a copy of the paper. Stash the paper here.

If a copier isn't readily available and you must make a special trip somewhere—down the hall, to another floor, to the quick-print shop—to use it, you can take the Photocopy file with you and take care of all your pending copying. Alternatively, this category of task could become a subcategory of your Errands file (see above).

TIP: CLEAR YOUR WRITE FILE

Here are some hints that will help you avoid procrastinating on your written correspondence:

- **Have note stationery on hand** so that you can jot a quick personal note. A handwritten note is a very powerful tool in this technical and frequently impersonal age.
- **Keep various kinds of greeting cards** available for quick and effective communication.
- **Write a reply** on the bottom of a letter and fax the response.
- **Ask yourself:** Would a phone call substitute for writing a letter?
- **Delegate your assistant** to draft the correspondence and you edit it.
- **Ask your assistant to address the envelope** for the note you plan to write and leave it on your desk. When I do this, I find that I feel responsible to my assistant for writing the note and completing the task.
- **Divide your Write file** into files for personal writing and business writing. I have a home office and I deal with both business and personal mail at my desk there. Having the two folders allows for flexibility: When I am going to the doctor's office, for example, I often take the "Write-Personal" file with me and jot a few notes to friends while I'm waiting for my appointment.
- **Block out a specific time** in your day to write. Just check your Write files to determine which letters you must write, rather than individually noting each letter in your calendar.

Read or Review

For most of us, this is the biggest action category, and everything you have to read will not fit in a file folder. I recommend implementing a "just-in-time" approach for reading—that is, file the information until you need or want to read it. This avoids my wasting my time by, say, reading an article now about purchasing new equipment and not acting on it for six weeks, when I won't remember what I read. For more on managing your Read or Review files, see the box on page 80. (If you use *Taming the Paper Tiger* software, you can keep entire magazines and use the computer to cross-reference articles of interest so you can find them when you want to read them.)

Scan

Combining into one file papers that you want to scan

will save you time or enable you to delegate the task.

Sign

One of my clients used to complain that he spent too much time on hold on the phone. His assistant complained that she couldn't get him to sign checks. So, she created a red file of things to sign, which she left by his phone: She got the checks signed, and he felt less frustrated because he could accomplish something while he was left on hold.

Take Home, or Take to Work

Designate a spot to put papers and other items that you need to take home. Choose a convenient location— under the credenza or beside your briefcase, for example. If you are not accustomed to keeping your briefcase in the same spot all the time, try it—and have a similar setup at home.

Write

Sometimes your next action will be to write a letter. This includes business letters, memos, thank-you notes, and special-occasion cards. If this is a problem area for you, take time to think about what you can do to make the task easier (see the box at left). You can include e-mail here or have a separate Action File for E-mail to Send.

Certainly word-processing is an enormous asset for dealing with this task. For example, if you write a thank-you note that you particularly like, and it fits a situation that's likely to arise again, file the letter in your computer under the category of form letters and an appropriate subcategory, such as "Thank You's."

Where to Put Action Files

So where do you put all these files? Well, it's a matter of personal preference, but accessibility is key. Some people prefer to keep them on top of their desks or in a nearby file drawer. I use a combination system: I open the file drawer in my desk as soon as I sit down, so those

TIP: HOLD YOUR ACTION FILES

Try these tools for containing folders that you keep on your desktop:

- **A variety of attractive holders** for hanging files that will sit on top of your desk or on a credenza—my favorite approach
- **A stairstep-type holder** that will hold manila files or files in your favorite color
- **A hot file**—a plastic holder that hangs on the wall or, if it has a magnetic back, on a file cabinet
- **The Pendaflex Mobile File System,** described on page 131 of Chapter 12.

files will be available for quick reference. Because my workstyle is to work on two or three major projects each day, I put those files in a hot-project tray on top of my desk. In any event, make sure that you can reach your Action Files—especially your most frequently used ones—from wherever you sit.

Create File Systems for Projects or Events

As I mentioned earlier, one method of sorting papers that require action is to divide them into categories by the name of a project or event—say, a trip or meeting. For example, as soon as I get the first piece of paper for an upcoming trip—a ticket, meeting announcement, and so on—I create an Action File for that trip. Here, I collect everything I plan to take with me, as well as reminders of things I want to pull from other files before I go. When the trip is over, I refile the information in the appropriate place. (If you use *Taming the Paper Tiger* software, note the file number on the paper for easy refiling.)

Sometimes, when a project is very large, I create an entirely separate filing system of Reference Files and Action Files for that project.

For example, suppose you are thinking of undertaking a big project, such as finding new building space. Instead of starting one file you know will be too small for the amount of material you'll collect, put whatever materials you have now in a pile on a bookshelf.

When you're ready to start the project, create your filing system for it. You may locate the project files in a section of your existing filing system, or set aside a separate drawer or container. If I have a temporary project that will be paper-intensive, such as chairing a committee, I use a portable plastic filebox under my desk. It provides easy access and doesn't take up valuable file space from my regular filing system.

As described previously, categorize the materials into:

- **Action Files** (for papers that require your action) by asking yourself: What's the next action I need to take on this piece of paper?
- **Reference Files** (for papers you may need for future reference): If I want this piece of paper again, what word will I think of?

In some cases, you may have only one Reference File and one Action File, while a very large project may require many Reference Files and many Action Files.

Keep in mind that in a paper system that is flowing effectively, an Action File can become a Reference File and vice versa. For example, an idea for a project that resides in your Reference Files can become an Action File when you're ready to move on it. When the project is completed, the Action Files once again become Reference Files. Or, at the beginning of a project, you may create an Action File for a specific phase of the project, and when that phase is over, you will retire the file to the Reference Files.

In my case, all project files are identified by the name of the client, whether it's a meeting planner, publisher, or a consulting client. It is an Action File and contains everything related to that client, as long as the file is manageable. If the file gets too bulky to manage, I create a Reference File to contain the historical papers I want to keep for that client.

TIP: KEEP YOUR E-MAIL ON PAPER OR ELECTRONICALLY?

In seminars, I often ask attendees, "How many of you print out your e-mail?" The vast majority raises their hands—timidly. But let's face it, sometimes paper is highly practical. Complex proposals, for example, often require discussions for which you need a printed copy that result in physical notes, making the electronic e-mail less valuable than the printed-out version.

On the other hand, printing out everything is not likely a good solution.

The key to managing e-mail is determining when to keep hard copy and when to keep electronic copy, keeping in mind that sometimes both may be practical. As in the case above, a printed version may have value for discussion, while the electronic version may have value for creating new versions after the discussion. In either event, the principles of the Paper Tiger methodology will improve communication and increase your productivity.

Apply Action Principles to Your E-Mail

Love it or hate it—or both—e-mail is increasingly the primary method for communicating in today's digital world—at work and at home. Let's look at how we can apply this discussion of Action Files to the information you receive via e-mail. As with paper, consistency is the key to managing e-mail—along with replying to your messages as soon as possible.

Manage Your In-Box

- **Whenever you open your incoming e-mail,** apply the FAT System (File-Act-Toss) to each message.
- **Apply my "2-Do Rule" whenever possible.** If you can reply in 2 minutes or less, then do so right away. It will take longer to file the message and retrieve it again than to "just do it!"
- **If you aren't sure you need it, toss it.** Unlike a paper wastebasket, you can always retrieve e-mail from electronic trash by using the "Find Message" feature available in most e-mail programs. (If the company empties the e-mail system's trash without your knowledge, create a folder on your computer called "my

trash," to which you move any messages that you would otherwise delete. I save these "trashed" messages for 6 months.)

- **To avoid an overflowing in-box of e-mail,** create folders. For example, you might have folders for each of the people who directly report to you, for each project, for a committee that you chair, and for subjects of particular interest. For example, I have a folder called "statistics," where I file e-mails with statistical information that I may want to recall for my media contacts.

- **For e-mail that takes more time to reply,** either leave it in the in-box or file it in an appropriate folder, such as "Action" or "Reply."

- **If you use permanent Action Files for managing your paper** (such as those for Call, Discuss, Online, and so on that I discussed earlier in this chapter), you can use them to file the paper copies of e-mails that require your action, such as "discuss with John."

- **For e-mail that you want to keep in the electronic format,** drag it to the appropriate folder as described in the first tip.

- **Many e-mail programs,** such as *Outlook Express,* allow you to set rules for your e-mail so that, for example, messages with certain words will go directly into designated folders.

- **If you need or want a paper copy of an e-mail** for future reference, print it out and file it in your paper-management system so that you can find it again in 5 seconds or less.

- **After you have finished with an e-mail folder** (say, one that you created for a specific project), you can store it on a floppy or Zip disk in case you need it later. Or perhaps your e-mail program or system has an archiving feature.

How I Handle My E-Mail

When I'm in the office, I generally check my e-mail first thing in the morning, at mid day and before I leave. When I travel, I typically check it at the end of the day only.

TIP: SEND E-MAIL YOUR RECIPIENTS WILL LOVE

- **Use the subject line** to clearly describe the topic of your e-mail. This is helpful for the recipient and for you if you want to find a message you've sent.
- **Include only one subject** per e-mail message. This method will greatly simplify e-mail filing and retrieval.
- **For a lengthy or complicated e-mail,** create the e-mail in your word processing program and then copy to your e-mail. If you suffer an e-mail glitch during the sending process, you can easily retrieve the content of your message and not have to recreate it from memory.
- **When replying** to any e-mail, attach enough of the old message for the recipient to remember the content of the original e-mail, but delete unnecessary information or duplication.
- **Avoid sending** e-mail attachments whenever possible. E-mail recipients are becoming more reluctant to open attachments due to the increasing prevalence of viruses that can infect one's computer system via opened attachments. Alternatively, you might send an attachment, but include the text of the attachment in the body of the e-mail, with the explanation that the attachment will have better formatting. That way the recipient can get the gist of the message without opening the attachment.
- **Consider using** your contact-management software (such as *ACT!*) to send all of your outgoing e-mail. With many such programs, you can not only send your e-mail, but attach copies of your outgoing e-mail messages to the recipients' contact records. For example, to send an e-mail to a client, I would go to her record in *ACT!,* click on "send e-mail," and my *Outlook Express* e-mail program will open. When I send the e-mail, I can save a copy of the outgoing e-mail in the client's record in *ACT.*

As I read each message, I decide which of three actions—file, act, or toss—I plan to take:

- **If the action is toss,** I delete it immediately.
- **If I can't reply immediately** because I don't know the answer or don't have the information I need, I print out a copy of the message so that I can keep track of it in my paper system. Just as I would with a piece of paper that arrives in my in-box, if the action is required at a specific time, I make a note in my calendar, or if it isn't, on my to-do list.
- **If I need to answer a message,** but, at the moment, I

don't have time or all the information I need, I file the message in my out-box. My program reminds me that I have messages in the out-box; I can't forget to handle them.

- **If I send a message** and want to make sure that I get a reply, I put a reminder in my calendar: "Heard from so-and-so regarding this or that?"
- **If the e-mail message** doesn't require any action, but I want to keep the information for future reference, I file it.
- **If the appropriate file**—whether computer or paper— already exists, I immediately file the message.
- **If I must create a file,** but I don't have time to do it right now, I leave the message in my in-box and return to it later.

Manage Your Voice Mail

The consistency rule that applies to e-mail applies to voice mail, too. The first step to dealing effectively with your voice mail is to identify a place to record the contents of your messages. If your calendar or planner has enough writing space, you may choose to makes notes about your voice-mail messages there. That's a strategy I used for many years, but it changed as the number of calls increased and I gained an assistant who could help me return them. Now, whoever listens to the message records it in a book on my desk and notes the initial of the person who is responsible for re-turning the call beside the message. When someone acts on the messages or the appropriate person re-ceives it, the message is crossed off the list.

The FAT principle applies to voice mail just as it does to hard copies and e-mail. Whenever possible, for a message that you want to act upon, make a note of it in your calendar or your phone record book and delete the message right away.

Does your voice-mail system allow you to forward messages to others? If so, you can use this feature as an alternative to my phone record-book strategy.

Your voice-mail system may allow you to file the

TOOL: READY FOR ACTION AT BARBARA'S DESK

TOP OF MY DESK
- **My calendar**
- **Spiral notebook** for recording voice-mail messages
- **In-box** for mail I haven't yet read
- **Out-box** for items to go to my assistant
- **To-file box** for items that will go to my Reference Files

RIGHT-HAND DESK DRAWERS
Permanent Action Files, including those for:
- **Calls**
- **Calls Expected**
- **Data Entry**
- **Discuss,** with a file for each person with whom I need to converse
- **E-mail to Send**

- **Errands**
- **Write,** subdivided into separate files for business and personal correspondence

MY ASSISTANT KEEPS
- **Pending Files,** with separate files for each month and one for the following year. My assistant gives me what I need at the appropriate time.
- **Temporary Action Files,** which are numbered 1 to 60 using the *Paper Tiger* software. I use these for projects that I'm currently working on.
- **Upcoming Speeches**, with a file for each speech. These are organized chronologically by the date of the speech.

message in an archive for future reference, for a number of days. There isn't much point to doing this unless you want to replay the message for someone else. Once the message is filed, it is likely to expire without your acting on it.

If you want to save a message that applies to a particular project, write it on a separate piece of paper, noting the date received, and file it in that project file. (When I am traveling, I carry a spiral-bound notebook to record voice-mail messages from my cell phone, as well as from my office phone, if my assistant isn't in.)

CHAPTER 9

Organize Your Computer

Besides having to organize the paper that results from our new technology, we now also have to organize the technology itself. Luckily, the principles are the same as those we've already discussed. Now lets look at how to apply them.

Your computer is basically an electronic filing cabinet—regardless of what kind of operating system your computer uses, what kind of graphical interface it has to show you how things are organized, what tools are available to you, and what kind of words or icons it uses to identify and describe those features.

Whether you use a PC or a Mac, the principles of organizing the programs and the information within are basically the same. PC and Mac users enjoy most of the same user-friendly file-management features. What does matter, to some extent, is the way the operating system shows you the file index that your computer generates and how it allows you to manipulate the index. I'll discuss more about these features later in the chapter.

Bottom-line, your computer-filing system can be set up very similarly to your paper-filing system. The box on the following pages shows the similarities between the two filing systems.

Set Up Your Filing System

If you have a computer full of files, and you spend more time than you can afford looking for the ones you need, the easiest way to get yourself out of the quagmire is to start over—just as we discussed for your paper-filing

TIP: COMPARE YOUR COMPUTER FILES WITH YOUR PAPER FILES

PAPER	COMPUTER FILES
Filing cabinet	**Hard disk** This is where you store your files, which contain documents and information, and your computer programs. The computer reads or accesses the information on the hard disk via the drive, just like playing a CD on a CD player.
Brief case	**A portable and removable data-storage medium** Such media include CD-ROM, Zip disks or removable tape cartridges. Your computer may have an A: drive, the slot on the front of the computer where you can insert and run a floppy disk, and it may have others.
Multiple filing cabinets	**Local-area network (LAN)** If your PC or Mac is networked, this means that your computer and all of the other computers on the system are connected to multiple drives in various locations so as to share the contents of the disk drives and the use of other components, such as printers, fax modems, tape back-ups, and so on.
File drawer	**File directory** This is where you keep all files in a single category. For example, you could keep all files related to your word-processing program in one file directory, or all files related

system. What does that mean? Ignore all your old files. Design your new computer-filing system, using the principles we will discuss. Then refile the old files into the new system as you need them or, whenever possible, delete them.

How do you design an effective computer-filing system? For one thing, you must remember one of the most important—and neglected—principles of organizing computer files: A computer's value is that it allows you to reuse a document. Sometimes you may simply want to print another copy. Other times, you may want to update or change the document in some way. But if you don't intend to use the document again, there's no value in storing it in a computer. If you need to keep a

	to a major project or client in another directory. *Note:* File directories and subdirectories (see below) in DOS and Windows are the equivalent of folders in Macintosh.
Hanging file	**File subdirectory** This is where you keep all files related to a single subcategory of the larger file directory. For example, the directory might be CLIENT X, while the subdirectory would be CLIENT X/LETTERS. If multiple people are using the same computer, you could have a directory for each user, who would in turn create subdirectories for their projects. You can create subdirectories several layers deep. For example: CLIENT X/LETTERS/SMITH/CAMPAIGN.
Interior/Manila file	**Computer file** This is where you keep a document or all documents related to a single subcategory of the subdirectory.
File label	**File name**
Piece of paper	**File** (word-processing document, spread sheet, presentation)
File index	**Windows Explorer, File Manager, and the Macintosh Desktop** These are visual ways of seeing all the programs that you have in your computer.

copy of a file's contents for reference, your alternatives are to keep a hard copy in your paper-filing system or a copy on a disk for the purposes of archiving.

Organize the Keepers

The first step to effectively organizing your computer is to place all the files you create into one directory, regardless of what program created those files. (This follows the same principle as filing paper information according to how you will use it, not where you got it.)

Microsoft Windows has a folder for that purpose called "My Documents." This will make it easier to retrieve what you need, regardless of what program created it, and make it easier to back it up for safekeeping.

TIP: FOR OPERATING SYSTEM HOLDOUTS

If you are using DOS or a pre-Windows '95 program, not only are you working with a nearly antique tool that is probably limiting your work capability, but you're also limited in naming your computer file to eight characters plus an extension of three characters. The extension identifies the program in which the file was created. Most programs automatically assign the extension, but some allow you to change the three letters for better identification. In Microsoft Word the extension is automatically .doc or .dot, while in WordPerfect, you can use the character extension to help identify the file, assigning, say, "LTR" for letter.

It's been my experience that in paper systems, people frequently get into trouble because they have too many categories, while in computer systems, they get into trouble because they have too few (i.e., directories and subdirectories).

Why are the two systems different? Because it's easier to flip through one manila file that has 20 pieces of paper in it than it is to go through ten files with two pieces of paper in each. In contrast, it's easier to scroll up and down a computer screen looking for directories and subdirectories than to open documents. In addition, your computer gives you a search capability that will help you find the file you want by searching for key words without having to actually open each file. Of course, you can ignore the option of creating subdirectories and keep all your files in one directory, but that would be like tossing all your tools in your garage and then spending hours looking for a screwdriver!

Categories That Reflect Your Work

The next step is to determine the major categories of your files. Those might include project or client names, geographical locations, or your professional and personal roles. For example, I have a directory entitled:

- **Taming1** for my first book. It has subdirectories for each chapter, as well as for book-related issues, such as marketing materials and pricing information.
- **CSA** for my role as a board member of the Carolina Speaker's Association. Because I keep very few docu-

ments related to CSA, I have not created any subdirectories for it.

- **Clients** for materials I've created for my clients. It has subdirectories for each client.

Some of my favorite directories are:

- **Pending,** for files on which you're currently working. You can quickly see which documents are in process, or if necessary, it will be easy for someone else to retrieve your work.
- **Out-box,** for work that you've completed, but need to print, fax, give to someone else, or send to another location later on—say, when you are working on your e-mail.
- **Home,** for information you need to take home.
- **Office,** for information you need to keep at the office.

Which Drive Is the Right One?

If you're working on a networked computer, you may have a choice of multiple drives or servers on which to file your documents. Your organization may already have made this decision for you. For example, all files of mutual business interest or used by a single division of the business may be filed on one drive or server to which everyone has been given access, while employees' private work files may be filed on another.

Don't make your strategy too complicated. It would, for example, probably be more confusing than helpful to send separate projects—or parts of projects—to separate drives or servers, when there's space for all of them in the same location, especially if they're all related to the same role or client in your work life or even if different departments are charged with different aspects of the project.

Name Your Files

In the old days, computer-file names were limited to eight characters. Fortunately, for most computer users, those days are over. Unfortunately, most of them don't take advantage of the fact to create meaningful and easily understood file names. You still may not use certain punctuation marks and symbols or spaces in file names.

continued on page 98

TIP: PAPER VERSUS COMPUTER FILING OPTIONS

Let's create a document in paper and on the computer. Say that you want to write a memo to your boss about developing a new brochure, and you want to keep a copy for your files. In each medium, we'll first look at how you're likely to handle the task, the consequences of that "strategy," and then at the better way, which guarantees that you'll be able to find the piece again when you need it.

THE PAPER-FILING WORLD

Creating the memo

You pull out a blank sheet of paper and handwrite or type the text of your memo, send the original and keep a copy for your files. Or, you write the memo in your word-processing program, print two copies—one to send and one to file—and don't bother to save the document on the computer.

What you might do

You toss your copy of the memo in your to-file box.

What happens next

You need your copy of the memo and you must go digging through your to-file box to find it.

The better way to file in the first place

At this point of filing your copy, ask yourself: If I want this piece of paper again, what word will I think of first? Check your file index to see if that file exists. If not, add it to the list. Note that word in the upper right-hand corner of your copy of the memo, so that you, or the person who does your filing, will know where to file it. Because you'll work on more than one publication at a time, you designate space in one of your file drawers for Publications and add it to the label on the outside of the file drawer. You create a hanging file, "Publication—XYZ," for the current brochure that you're working on. As you create other documents related to the XYZ brochure, you add them to the front of the existing file in order as they are sent. If the file becomes too thick to manage, you subdivide the file into smaller categories, such as "XYZ—Price Estimates" and "XYZ—Proofs."

Note: If you are using an operating system and versions of software that allow for long file names, try naming your files with a series of words that will help you retrieve the information you want. For example, if I am writing an article on organizing for taxes, I can save the file to: Organizing Your Taxes, article, XYZ client, ABC publication, editor's name, date (up to 255 characters). When I want to find the file again, I can use my computer's "Find File," function and type in any of the words that I used, and I—or someone else—can quickly find it.

THE COMPUTER-FILING WORLD

Creating the memo

You open up your word-processing program and type your memo on the blank screen presented to you for a new document. You print out one copy to send and keep a copy in the computer for future reference.

What you might do

In a rush, you tell the program to save and close the document, but don't bother to name it yourself. Your word-processing program does the job for you, naming the document something meaningless like "doc2.doc," (in *Word),* which indicates that this is the second document you've neglected to name in this program. *(Note:* Some programs, such as *WordPerfect,* will not allow you to close a document without giving it a specific file name.)

What happens next

You need your copy of the memo and you must scrounge through your file directory, looking for a file name that rings a bell. Completely ignoring those anonymous "doc.docs," you give up.

The better way to file in the first place

When you're done writing any document, you save it to a particular drive (if you have more than one drive, you'll have to decide which one) and to the subdirectory of the program that you used to create the file. Then you name the file using keywords and phrases separated by commas. You can reorganize files into new directories or subdirectories by using the drag-and-drop feature or the move command.

TIP: REVISIT YOUR COMPUTER-FILE INDEX

Unlike the File Index for your file cabinets, your computer-file index is automatically generated for you and updates itself every time you create a new file, directory or subdirectory. However, it's still a good idea to revisit your computer-file index periodically to see if it still reflects your needs.

In *Microsoft Word*, don't overlook the "Summary" feature, which allows you to list additional information and key words to help you find the file.

To determine how to name a file, use the same technique we discussed for paper files. Ask yourself: If I want this file again, what word will I think of first? Key in that word first. Now add other words or phrases that might help you retrieve that file. Separate the identifying words with commas (punctuation that is allowed).

In order to prevent having too many files in one folder, I create a folder for each program or project, such as Word, Excel, Act!, Papertiger. When I want to save a file, I first choose the appropriate folder, and then name the file with a title and keywords. For example, I would file an article that I've written under: C:/MyDocuments/Organizing Your Tax Records, article, (name of publication), (name of editor), and (date). Then, when I need to write another article, I do a search (Start Menu, Find File—or Search) and type in the word "article." In a few seconds, I have every article in my computer, which makes it easier to update an old article or combine parts of several articles, thus eliminating the need to create completely new work and saving lots of time.

Clean Out Your Computer

Keeping your hard drive free of unwanted files is a good idea, especially if you have a laptop or a smaller disk drive. Consider deleting:

- **Files containing working drafts** of documents that have since been completed.

TIP: PREVENT CRASHES

All the organization in the world will be worthless if your computer crashes. To minimize that possibility, be sure that you regularly scan and defrag your computer. With a Windows operating system, you will find this function under: Start Programs, Accessories, System Tools, Disk Clean-Up and Disk Defrag. If your computer's operating system doesn't provide for this, you can buy a utility program, such as *Norton Utilities,* that will.

- **Empty files** that you created but never used or from which you moved material.
- **Files by different names** that contain the same material.
- **Files containing material** that is outdated, can't be reused, or you know you will never need again.

Be careful, however, not to remove any files that are essential to the running of the computer or a program that you wish to continue using, such as those ending with the extensions .exe or .dll.

You can copy all files that you want to keep for reference to disks, which you can organize using the suggestions given beginning on page 103. Although the file index in Windows or on the Macintosh would typically be alphabetized by file name, you can alternatively specify that they be sorted by type (that is, by the program that created it, represented by the file extension), size (amount of computer disk space taken up), or—most importantly for our purposes here—by the date that it was created or last worked on and saved. So you could, for example, sort by date and review only those files last revised six months ago or longer. You could then copy those files that you wanted to save for reference to floppy disks and delete the rest from the hard disk.

If your computer is networked, storage capacity may not be an issue. If it is, chances are that your network's system manager will have to monitor the network's storage capacity and will initiate a computer File Clean-Out Day if the system is approaching its limits. It's either that or buy new additional storage.

Backing up is easy enough to do, but like all organizing tasks, you have to remember to do it—regularly.

Back Up and Prevent Disaster

Can you imagine what would happen if some very strong person up-ended your filing cabinet so that all your files and papers fell in a heap on the floor? Your papers could end up scrambled beyond recognition, or some of them could slide under the furniture and you'd never find them again. While this is only remotely possible with your file cabinets, it's far more likely with your computer. If a hard disk crashes, you could lose months' worth of work or only partially recover it—to say nothing of what it would do to your blood pressure!

It's usually just a matter of time before your computer crashes. Therefore, backing up the information on it is an essential organizing task. By backing up, you will:

- **Protect against data loss.** If a data loss occurs, you can simply restore your data, eliminating the need to rekey and reconstruct.
- **Archive data.** Backing up provides an effective method for storing seldom-used files and for long-term storage. It also allows you to easily transfer data between home and work.
- **Increase system performance.** Performing a total disk backup, erasing the disk, and restoring from back-up media to disk reduces file fragmentation, which increases processing speed. You can also increase system performance by storing offline data that you do not use regularly. Because the system does not have to read through as many files on your hard drive, it can access information more quickly.

When and How Much to Back Up

Backing up is easy enough to do, but like all organizing tasks, you have to remember to do it—regularly. How often is often enough depends on how much you value your time and how critical your work is. Backing up once a week might be enough for some people, but if you're working on a critical project where mere hours count, then you might want to back up those project files every few hours.

Similar considerations will determine how much of

your material you choose to back up. You might choose one of the following strategies:

- **Total back up.** You save all files and directories on the drive that you specify.
- **Selective back up.** You choose specific files and directories to back up. Selection is possible at any level, whether directories, subdirectories, or individual files. With this option it's simple to transfer data to other sites or to archive selected files for storage.
- **Incremental or modified back up.** You back up only those files that have been changed since your last back up.

Choose the Back-Up Media

Some people copy all their files from the hard disk to a bunch of floppy disks. Although back-up programs make this task easier, it's still a time-consuming chore. Who wants to spend half an hour backing up computer files after finishing work? The best way to do this is with a high-capacity back-up option—such as a CD-RW and drive, a Zip disk and drive, or online back-up sites—and good back-up software. Windows operating systems come with the Microsoft back-up function, but there are others on the market. Since updates and changes in this field are rampant, we have resisted the temptation to actually list the individual products and companies, but a quick keyword search on the Internet will lead you to the newest technology. In addition, if you compress your files with a compression program, they will require less storage space for backup; the most popular of these is *WinZip* (www.winzip.com), which offers a free trial version, but there are others.

The Importance of Labeling

Don't forget to label your back-up media. First, label diskettes in pen with the user's name and the day of the week (for disks 1-5) and "off site" (for disk 6). Second, fill in the diskette number and date in pencil so that you can update the information the next time you use that series of diskettes.

Here's a sample of the label from my back-up tape:

> H + A BACKUP — MONDAY
> Tape #____1____ of ___5___ Date:_10/30/01_

Your Software

It's wise to keep a file of all the original software disks for the computer programs that you use. If your computer crashes, you will be able to easily reinstall the programs you need. Even if your computer comes with programs already installed on the hard disk, you should still receive the original disks for the software or be able to make back-up copies yourself from the program. Keep your backup off-site or in a fireproof safe.

If You're on a Network

If your computer is networked, you probably don't have to worry about backing up your files for safekeeping. That's because most networks are backed up regularly by the system administrator or automatically by the network itself. But before you assume that this is the case, check with your system administrator to find out about your company's back-up practices. You'll want to know the following:

■ **How often is the system backed up?** If it is backed up every other day, are you willing to lose two days' of your work?

TIP: MORE ABOUT BACKING UP

The key to protecting your data is routine backup and rotation of whatever medium you are using to ensure that you can restore selected files or an entire hard drive or server as needed. How you back up depends on the number of daily changes you make and your need for historical data.

No matter which media you choose (floppy disk, CD-RW, or magnetic tape),

you should always have at least two sets of back-up data and alternate using them, so that if one set is damaged, the other is available. Be sure to label your backup clearly.

Finally, make sure to store your backup separately from your computer. If your computer is stolen, or the sprinkler system comes on, your backup will be useless.

- **If the system crashes, how long would it be before you'd again have access to the documents you need?** A few hours' delay may not be a problem, but a day or two when you're on deadline may be a big problem— in which case, again, you need to be backing up your critical files yourself.
- **Which of the programs that you use are installed for everyone's benefit on the network?** Which programs are installed locally in your computer and wouldn't automatically be reinstalled on the network after a system crashed? Be sure to keep back-up copies of those programs.

Avoid the Tomb of the Unknown Diskettes

Ever had one of those exasperating moments when you need something and realize that you must search through a pile of outdated, mislabeled, unidentified and disorganized disks or tapes to find it? As with many organizing tasks, the solution isn't complicated—it just requires consistency. It will be much easier to retrieve information if you use that basic organizing principle: Put like things together.

- **For starters,** put all your program disks together in one container and all your back-up disks in another. (It is easier to retrieve disks from one large container rather than several small ones.)
- **If you are using CDs,** you can save space by throwing away the jewel cases they come in, and store them in larger cases. A zipper case holds 100 CDs and is great for traveling.
- **On disks or tapes,** label with non-smear markers for permanent labels, or with pencil for information that will change, such as a date.
- **Identify a specific location** where you can collect disks or tapes that you can reuse. Avoid confusion by making sure they're empty before you stow them.

TIP: WHEN YOU BUY NEW SOFTWARE

- **Put all software diskettes or CDs** in one place, along with the manuals and registration forms. You can discard the original boxes if they don't work for you. Before you do, though, tear off the proof of purchase for potential discounts on future upgrades.
- **Register the software** according to the manual.
- **Determine what customer support** is available, and make sure to record the appropriate contact information, including your customer number whenever one is assigned, in your card file or

your contact-management database.
- **If you no longer use an outdated software program,** remove it from your computer and discard the manuals and support information from your office. Observe any appropriate precautions, as described in the software manual.
- **Install new software** programs one at a time. If you install several at once, without rebooting as part of the installation, and there's a defect in one of the programs, it will be difficult to determine which program caused the problem.

Preserve Your Privacy

It's unlikely that people would walk in and nose around in the file cabinets in your office, and even if they were likely to, you could probably keep them out with a simple lock on the cabinet. Similarly, if you keep top secret or personal files on your computer, share a computer with someone (including a home computer on which you work and other family members play), or work on a networked computer, you might want to give some files passwords.

If you password-protect any of your files, don't take chances on committing the passwords to memory. You'll waste your time and experience frustration if you try to open a file and realize that you can't remember the password. One option is to keep a file card labeled "passwords" in your card file, and write all your passwords on it. If that location isn't private enough, you'll have to find one that is—and commit the location to memory.

A Note About Groupware

Lotus Notes is the most famous software in a relatively new category of products known as groupware—or project-management software—that allows individual computer users to be a part of a group and share information. This software can help you do the following:

- **Create databases** and specify who can see the information. This can be one person, everyone in a department or the entire company.
- **Ensure that all company forms are standard.** All company forms will be online, which will make you look much more organized.
- **Back up all information** and keep it safe.
- **Derive information** from many different sources and keep it in *Lotus Notes*.
- **Facilitate communication** by working with all of the most popular operating systems. *Lotus Notes* supports Microsoft Windows, Apple Macintosh, IBM OS/2, and Unix.
- **Reduce the barriers of geography.** All employees can be connected and share in discussions and news, access vital corporate data, and so on, regardless of their location.

Lotus Notes is so powerful because it becomes a central repository for information that the company wants to keep and continually use. The software can be used for reference and workflow. It has excellent formatting and searching capabilities. It not only handles internal company communications well but also facilitates communications to the outside world through e-mail and fax.

As a holding tank for the vital information of the organization, groupware has many uses. Some companies use *Lotus Notes* to minimize paper and facilitate keeping information current, such as policies and procedures. Others organize their information by department in *Lotus Notes,* so that it can be shared and accessed 24/7. This reduces the number of meetings to share information and provides better communication between departments as a project progresses.

Because of its sophisticated features, *Lotus Notes* has quickly become the standard by which all groupware products are measured. Groupware has become a popu-

A good contact database with notes can eliminate thick file folders of information and faded Post-it Notes to which you have become oblivious.

lar way for companies to get more organized. These products, when implemented properly, can help the organization use the various information collected every day and more easily reach its objectives.

Use a Contact-Management Program?

My tool of choice in contact management is *ACT!* Because of *ACT!* I can eliminate all those elusive business cards I collect and be confident that I will give the right person the right information at the right time. Scraps of papers, Post-it Notes, and reminders scribbled on napkins can be transformed from annoyances into action—at exactly the right time. Now, don't get me wrong! I can't imagine living without Post-it Notes, but they were designed to be a temporary tool—not a faded reminder permanently stuck to your computer monitor and to which you become oblivious.

With *ACT!*, not only can I be sure that I am doing the right thing at the right time, but because my support staff and I are networked, I can easily check to see what they have done, too. For example, let's say I answer the phone and the caller is someone whose name I don't recognize. I can quickly do an *ACT!* search and know that my assistant talked to this person last week about a potential presentation. I note in *ACT!* what have I said to the prospect in this conversation, and set an *ACT!* alarm for my assistant to send the appropriate additional information. Here's another example: I frequently receive e-mail newsletters from experts in various fields. I put their contact information in *ACT!* so that I can access their expertise in a matter of seconds.

Another favorite tool of mine in this arena is *Card Scan* (www.cardscan.com), which enables you to scan business cards into *ACT!*, eliminating the need to type in the info. If you collect ten or more business cards in a week, it's well worth the investment. It's a not a perfect system, for sure, but it is a major time and frustration saver.

Remember: A good contact database with notes can eliminate thick file folders of information.

Do You Need a Financial-Management Program?

In my experience, one of the biggest nagging worries in the back of many entrepreneurial minds is the possibility of being audited. Using a financial program, such as *QuickBooks*, eliminates that worry. While *QuickBooks* won't reduce the possibility of an audit, in the even of one, it will increase one's comfort with the ability to easily produce accurate information.

QuickBooks (or *QuickBooks Pro* for time-billing companies) lets the business owner easily keep a finger on the fiscal pulse of the company. The owner of a successful business must have a working knowledge of the financial-management routine and develop a system of frequent checks on the growth and health of the business.

While *QuickBooks* has remarkably vast capability, the real secret to successful money management—at work or at home—is simplicity. By designing the *QuickBooks* accounting system to match the flow and style of the business, one can easily enter day-to-day transactions, including customer and vendor invoices, bank account transactions, payroll, and inventory. While most business owners are naturally inclined to overclassify in terms of the number of income and expense categories available, a better strategy is to use fewer accounts. Those that roughly correspond to the tax return (perhaps restated in the language of the user's business), with a few additions specific to the enterprise should be sufficient. Then, when it is time to do those infrequent analyses of rare events, *QuickBooks'* comprehensive capability for sorting into subcategories (i.e. payee, date, transaction type, etc.) comes into play.

Once the data-entry system becomes routinized, the owner will want to develop a few regular reports—snapshots of the business that allow him or her to see both the trigger points of the financial profile as well as the big picture, all at a glance. In this way the entrepreneur can remain in control of the direction of the business—past, present and future—avoiding unseen potholes along the way.

And guess what? The new version of *QuickBooks* interfaces with *ACT!* to make it easy when it's time to convert all those contacts into paying customers!

Should You Store Paper on Paper or Electronically?

Only a small portion of the information that exists on paper today is worth converting to a computer-readable format. However, as the quantity of information received and generated by businesses increases, electronic-storage options become more attractive.

There are basically two approaches to saving information electronically from its original paper form:

- **Scanning in paper documents** and storing them as images. Those files can be viewed using a variety of viewing tools, such as Adobe's popular *Acrobat Reader* (www.adobe.com), which converts any document to a portable document format (or .pdf) file that can be viewed by any computer, PC or Macintosh.
- **Scanning in documents** and converting their contents to computer-readable format—that is, text—using optical character-recognition (OCR) software.

Once the files have been created there's the issue of how to store them. Optical recording technologies, such as CD-ROM disks, are cheaper, while magnetic storage using hard drives allows for faster retrieval.

What kind of electronic storage you choose will depend at least in part on factors such as:

- **Whether your documents** are color or black-and-white
- **How many documents** you handle daily
- **Whether your documents** are written by hand or computer-printed.

The obvious advantage to electronic storage is saving space. Speed of access and retrieval is also a major benefit. It can be particularly attractive, for example, when electronic customer-information records are interfaced with a telephone system that identifies callers. Even if you have to type a customer's name before retrieving the file, the increase in customer-service effectiveness can be remarkable.

Other records, such as expense reports, invoicing, credit reports, and other documents relating to customer accounts are obvious candidates for electronic storage.

The downside? If the system is too difficult to learn or too slow to respond or maneuver in, employees will quickly retreat to paper.

The biggest threat to electronic storage of information is the viability of digital-storage media, such as CDs, whose lifetime isn't always guaranteed. (Hence, some companies' practice of backing up the backups every few years.)

Not to mention, remember all those 5 ¼-inch floppy disks for which we have no hardware? The possible obsolescence of media and technologies also presents a big challenge.

However, the biggest hurdles for most companies are the costs of obtaining and installing equipment and training, and the time necessary for implementation.

In my experience, the answer is a carefully managed approach using the best attributes of electronic and paper storage. The more effectively a company learns to manage paper, the easier and more cost-effective it will be to move to electronic storage.

One of the big advantages of electronic storage can become a disadvantage, as Bill Gates learned when he was called to account for messages sent to his e-mail box years previously. The issue of how long to keep personal information, such as bank statements and expired

> **The more effectively a company learns to manage paper, the easier and more cost-effective it will be to move to electronic storage.**

TIP: FOR MOBILITY'S SAKE

Consider backing up all your data on a portable hard-disk drive, so that you can carry it with you. This ensures that you will always have all the files you need when and where you need them.

insurance policies, triggered the first edition of *Taming the Paper Tiger* in 1988. I quickly learned that most businesses faced the same dilemma. Employees are scared to throw anything away, because the boss might ask for it, and many bosses were afraid—or don't take the time—to make a decision about records retention. Even when they do, the decision often breaks down in the implementation.

Paper is here to stay—at least for the foreseeable future. Research shows that introducing e-mail into a company increases paper printing by 40%. Let's face it: The portability of paper often makes it more desirable. A printout of a complex e-mail message that requires thinking, generates conversations in meetings, and results in handwritten notes is frequently far more valuable than the original electronic document. On the other hand, the ability to send information electronically and to let the users determine when and if to print out the information, offers the best of both worlds.

One financial-management company spent an immense amount of effort to develop and produce an incredibly valuable policies and procedures manual, which ended up in dusty binders on employee shelves. Today it resides on their wide-area network, where it is easily accessible at a moment's notice and always up-to-date.

Before this book makes it into your hands, new technologies will be available to store and easily retrieve electronic information. But don't put the cart before the horse. Making the decision of whether to go fully electronic or continue using paper should come after a careful analysis of what information is important to you and your company and in what form it will be most useful to you.

CHAPTER 10

Maintain Your Filing System

No matter how much time and energy you spend to create a filing system that fits your needs, you'll still need to adopt a plan to maintain the system. The following steps will help you:

Continually practice the Art of Wastebasketry. Take steps to limit the amount of space you need for file storage. This is especially important in these days of modular offices, frequent office reorganizations, and computers—especially nonnetworked PCs.

Clean out whenever you can. When you have a file in your hand or a directory on your computer screen, take an extra minute to eliminate whatever you know is unnecessary—even if you can't do it perfectly. I can't count how many times I've seen clients, holding something they knew they could toss, stop and say, "I'll have to clean this out someday," and promptly put it back in the file instead of directly into the wastebasket. Perfectionism may have a place, but this isn't it!

Define specific retention guidelines—whenever possible. Put that information on the File Index, or even on the file label itself. For example, "XYZ Newsletter: Keep l year."

Determine who will do the filing and when. If the filing system is well-designed, even temporary employees who know little about your business can actually do the filing.

Remember that filing something will never be any easier than it is today, and with every day that you wait, it will become more difficult.

If you are the only one capable of doing it, make an appointment with yourself to do it—every Friday or when the to-file box gets full.

Establish an annual File Clean-Out Day. Choose a time when your work schedule is likely to be less hectic—around the holidays, for example. For the self-employed person, try scheduling this task for just after tax time, when you're still familiar with your files but not overwhelmed with tax preparation. Or you could just wait until you need the file space. As long as you have room to file papers easily, purging isn't a major issue. But if you neglect filing because it's downright impossible to get your fingers into the file cabinet or you spend precious time scrolling up and down your computer screen looking for a file, then it's time for a File Clean-Out Day (see Chapter 16).

The Importance of the File Index

Make sure that the index remains a living document. If you're using your word-processing program to create your File Index, make notations on a printed copy when you add or delete a file, and then periodically update the index in your computer and print out clean copies. (If you use *Taming the Paper Tiger* software, print out the Retention Worksheet Form to make file cleaning a snap.) If you make an index, put it in a drawer and forget about it, you're very likely to forget the file titles you chose and make a file for "personnel" when you already have one called "employees." If that happens, you'll end up back where you started from in no time.

Stumbling Blocks to Success

Few people enjoy filing, and most of us procrastinate before doing it—sometimes for a long time. Even people who are paid to file sometimes let their to-file box overflow. People who should know better delay creating appropriate places to file their computer files and assigning them accordingly. Why? Well, here are a few of the most important reasons:

Sometimes, you just don't want to file. The consequences of procrastinating may not be so bad when you're dealing with paper; chances are, you have an idea of which pile to look in if you need something. But on your computer, if you don't actively decide where to file something when you save and close it, your computer will make the decision for you and file it in the last place in which you were working. The result is a misfiled document that, if you have any quantity of files in your system, will be really hard to find again. Say you write a memo about office reorganization, but you save it in a directory related to new business. Next time you look for the computer copy of the memo, you probably won't have a clue where to find it, and you will waste precious time searching through your many directories for it. And that assumes that you gave your memo a file name that you'll recognize (or a name or key words that you'll remember if you use a search function).

Filing can be time-consuming. This is particularly true if the filing system is poorly organized and you've let a lot of stuff accumulate. Many people give up and just leave those piles of paper in a box to deal with later. (And that, believe it or not, may be the best strategy—see the discussion of dealing with your backlog beginning on page 28.) Some people even leave a multitude of electronic project files—working drafts, final versions, memos, tables, and so on—languishing in their computers, hidden behind file names that made sense when they were being used, but have become mysterious with time. Remember that filing something will never be any easier than it is today, and with every day that you wait, it will become more difficult.

You may not know how to file things so you can find them again. That might help explain the first two stumbling blocks, too. Reading this book will provide the solutions to that problem.

No job is finished until the paperwork is done. After you've finished the fun part of a project, a meeting, or a trip, you've got to cope with the information you've accumulated. You'll find that you'll be more willing to file—and it will take less time—when you know how. The results of having a filing system that works are positive and long-lasting—and well worth the effort.

PART 3

Organizing in Special Situations

CHAPTER 11

When You Work From Home

M ore people are discovering the many pleasures—and challenges—of working in a home office. Most of them are entrepreneurs, but following the events of September 11, 2001, and ongoing corporate downsizing, an increasing number of employees spend all or part of their working hours at home. When I first started working out of my own home office, I did everything I could to hide the fact. Today, I can proudly bring clients to my home office.

A Real Office for Real Work

J ust having a home office isn't enough to guarantee that you'll get work done there. If you haven't designed your space to suit your needs and personality, with the right tools in the right places, your productivity and peace of mind will suffer. Obviously, your budget will guide many of the decisions that you make regarding your home office, but even if your capital is limited, you have numerous possibilities for creating a suitable workspace.

Consider Your Comfort

The first step is to choose a comfortable place to work, and most importantly, a place you enjoy. If you like sunshine or are allergic to mold, the basement probably won't work for you. I once was hired by a woman who had a beautiful custom-built home with a well-designed office that, she reluctantly admitted, she rarely used.

TIP: MOST COMMON MISTAKES

Here are the most common mistakes of working from a home office:
- **Wrong location** in the home
- **Lack of dedicated space** for work
- **Inappropriate furniture** and equipment
- **Lack of filing space**
- **A filing system** that doesn't work
- **Shortage of book** and storage space
- **An excess of clutter.** This can be a problem in any office, but it's more tempting at home—particularly if you're a keeper and short on space. I'm not suggesting that a pristine environment makes a better workspace, but many people have too much stuff in the areas where they're trying to work. Memorabilia, in particular, can become distracting when there's too much of it. Identify a particular place or memorabilia in your office, and when that place becomes full, decide whether to toss it, move it, or put it in storage.

When I walked into her home, I immediately understood why. From her dining room table, where her papers were spread, she faced a window that overlooked a beautiful lake, while from her desk, she viewed a cluttered bulletin board.

Pay Attention to Your Furniture

The roll-top desk you inherited from your grandfather may be gorgeous, but it could spell disaster if you have difficulty keeping track of papers in it or don't have room for your computer and keyboard on it. Furniture that is functional and comfortable is essential. Your desk is crucial to your work. For most people, the bigger the desk, the better. An L-shape is preferable, especially if you're using a computer. Most people find it easier to organize their work area if the desk has at least one file drawer.

Good-Quality Filing Cabinets Are Essential

Two-drawer lateral files that create counter space for

FROM MY FILES: THE WORK-AT-HOME CHALLENGE

When you work at home, often the biggest challenge in staying organized and managing your time is convincing others that you're working! Assertive behavior is essential. If a friend calls to chat about personal business at 10:00 A.M., politely say, "I'm in the middle of a work project right now. May I call you this evening?"

Don't try to be a supervising parent and a professional at the same time. Consider hiring a teenage neighbor or senior citizen to provide daycare, whether in your home or theirs. (Consult your accountant about any possible tax implications.) If you must work while your children are at home, explain what you are doing as clearly as you can and establish some physical sign to indicate when you are working and they are not to disturb you except in emergencies. A closed door works wonders. Finally, make a commitment to spend specific time with your children and honor your promise.

equipment, such as a photocopier and fax machine, are often a very practical use of space. One client who used her dining room for an office purchased beautiful wooden filing cabinets that matched her Scandinavian furniture and could be used as a side table for serving food when she had guests.

If your home office is too small to accommodate all the file cabinets that you need, locate them elsewhere in the house, and put a to-file box on or near your desk to gather papers that you'll take to the cabinets.

As a last resort, consider off-site storage, but only for those Reference Files that you are least likely to use. You don't want to have to run down to the storage center very often. Besides, if those files are expendable enough that you'd consider placing them in off-site storage, think about disposing of them altogether, unless they have long-term tax or other legal implications. By all means, avoid using an off-site location to store postponed decisions. Make sure that the storage space is worth what it costs you. (You can use *Taming the Paper Tiger* software to locate off-site resources in seconds.)

Phoning From and Away From Home

Having enough telephone lines and selecting the right

FROM MY FILES: MY NUMBER FOLLOWED ME

Through the wonders of technology I kept the same telephone number for 17 years, even though I had a home office in six locations in two states. When I first started my business in Virginia, I didn't have anyone to answer my phone when I was out and I wanted a Washington, D.C., telephone number, so I used a Washington, D.C., phone-answering service. When I hired someone to work in my home office in Virginia and answer my phone, I call-forwarded the D.C. number there. Callers thought they were talking to someone in Washington, D.C., but, in fact, we were in Virginia. Several years later, I moved to North Carolina, but I wanted to keep my Washington, D.C., presence, so I attached voice-mail service to the D.C. number and checked the voice-mail box daily. I kept the D.C. number for five years, until the volume of calls to it was insignifcant. Now, my business has an 800 number.

equipment and service features are also important home-office issues.

NUMBER OF PHONE LINES. Although technology now makes it possible to use one phone line for different purposes, such as multiple recipients whose calls are distinguished by different rings, fax machines, and online services, most home businesses need a minimum of two lines—one for personal use and one for business. If you're frequently online, you may need a dedicated line for your computer. You can use your personal line for your fax and outgoing calls (for which you can also use your cell phone), so that you don't tie up your business line when customers are trying to reach you.

Many people who have a home office need more than one business line—particularly if clients call frequently. To determine how many lines you really need, consider how many phone-related activities might happen at once:

- **Is more than one person** likely to be in your office at the same time?
- **Do you have a separate fax machine** or an internal fax on your computer?

- **Do you use online services? Frequently?** For extended periods of time? Is a phone line your only option for connection, or can you obtain cable-modem or DSL service in your area?

CORDLESS EQUIPMENT. When selecting telephone equipment, you may find cordless phones convenient, but make sure you don't sacrifice the quality of sound. Aside from your need to communicate easily and well, you don't want to suggest to clients that when you're working at home, you're working second-rate.

SERVICE FEATURES. One major phone-related issue is coverage of phone calls: What happens if you can't answer the phone and you have no one to back you up? Consider such features as:

- **Voice mail** to capture messages when you're on another call or away. You can set up multiple voice-mail boxes if you like, say, for different departments or staff members. If you have a single phone line, you can set up a mailbox for your family and one for your business. You'll be able to check your incoming messages and change your outgoing message from an off-site location when you're traveling.
- **Call waiting** to allow you to answer a second call as your first caller waits for you to return.
- **Call forwarding** so that calls to your office will ring on your cell phone or in another location.
- **Caller ID** so that you can see who has called you even if they didn't choose to leave a message.

You can purchase your own equipment or choose a voice-mail service provided by your telephone company (look under "Business Services" in your local phone book) or a separate company (look under "Telephone Answering Service" in the commercial listings). You'll probably be offered various packages of features. You'll have to decide which combination is worth your money.

In addition to your regular number, you may wish to provide your clients with a toll-free number. This can be a separate line, or for a few additional dollars each

While being responsive to your customers is a good thing, becoming a slave to your technology is not in the interest of your personal well-being in the long run.

month, you can have your toll-free calls ring right on your regular line.

Cell phones and pagers are becoming standard equipment among business owners. You might also consider a "follow me" service that allows you to have one number that rings in multiple places so you can be found anywhere, anytime. Here's how the service works: You enter each phone number with the period of time during which you will be available there. For example, you might enter your home phone number from 7:00 A.M. to 1:00 P.M., your cell phone number from 1:00 P.M. to 1:30 P.M., and a client's office number from 1:30 P.M. to 4:00 P.M. You can also block accessibility to any number for a period of time.

But be careful. While being responsive to your customers is a good thing, becoming a slave to your technology is not in the interest of your personal well-being in the long run. You can set your limits. For instance, I have a cell phone, but the number is not printed on my business card.

The Basics of Home-Office Equipment

Your Computer

In this day and age, a home office without a computer would be like a car without an engine. That doesn't necessarily mean that you have to have the latest and greatest. That would be an endless game, because it's nearly impossible to keep pace with technological advances.

However, don't do yourself a disservice in the long run so that you can save money in the short run. Whatever computer you purchase should have enough memory and speed to run the software that you need to do your job efficiently. And it's smart to purchase the most equipment you can afford, so that you can keep up with new versions of your software without having to purchase every new generation of hardware.

To determine what you really need, first identify

TIP: BEFORE YOU BUY OFFICE EQUIPMENT

Here are ten questions to ask before you buy any office equipment.

- **What is my primary incentive** for buying this equipment? What will I be able to do that I can't do now?
- **Will the equipment pay off** in terms of increased productivity or reduced stress?
- **Can I afford not to have this equipment,** or will my clients or associates interpret my failure to have it as a lack of professionalism?
- **Will this equipment become the standard** that everyone expects, so that I can't be without it?
- **Is there a cheaper way** to accomplish the same thing?
- **Would it be more cost-effective** to lease the equipment?
- **Is the equipment fast enough—** or much more than I really need or can afford?
- **Do I have the physical space** that the equipment requires?
- **How will I learn** to use it?
- **What additional services do I want** or need to purchase with this equipment (for example, a maintenance contract, additional telephone lines, or training or consulting services)?

what kind of activities are important to you and where you'll do them:

- **If you do most of your work in the office,** a desktop computer will be fine.
- **If you do most of your work outside the office,** or you want to be able to work in other locations, you may need a laptop computer.
- **If someone else will be working in your office,** you may need more than one computer.
- **Identify the software that's critical to your work** and make sure that whatever computer you choose will accommodate it and allow you to work efficiently.

The next question is: Do your computers need to be networked? Do they need to talk to each other, or can you use each computer for specific activities, and transfer information from one computer to another by diskette when necessary?

Keep in mind that the purchase of the machine is a small percentage of the actual cost of owning a computer. You must also pay for software and other equipment

TIP: DON'T SKIMP ON SUPPLIES

Be sure to have all the office supplies that you need. A quick recipe for panic—and increased cost—is discovering that you're out of letterhead stationery in the middle of printing a major proposal. Here are four tips for avoiding this dilemma:

- **Always have extra toner cartridges** on hand for printers and copy machines.
- **Keep a running shopping list of supplies** that you need to purchase. Make a note when you use the next-to-the-last-package of printer paper, so that you don't have to make emergency shopping trips.
- **Keep the list in an easily accessible place,** such as your Action File for errands, or posted inside the door of the supply closet.
- **Make sure anyone else who works with you** knows where the shopping list is—and uses it. Assign someone to shopping or ordering duty.

you may need, as well as costs incurred in setting up and learning the system. Although you may be able to do that by using books and manuals, you may find it easier—and cheaper in the long run—to hire a computer consultant. He or she can help you purchase and set up a system that meets your needs, provide you with training, propose and install upgrades when appropriate, troubleshoot, and generally help you avoid a lot of personal and professional teeth-grinding.

Fax Machines

Because I send and receive several faxes per day, I prefer a freestanding fax machine with a dedicated phone line. I purchased a fax machine with a telephone handset, so that I can use it as an additional telephone when I have a temporary employee working in the office. If most of the faxes you send will be created on your computer, a modem and a fax software package may be all you need. I use both methods.

A Copy Machine

The first piece of office equipment I purchased was a copy machine—and I've never been sorry. One of my favorite networking activities is sending copies of favorite articles to clients or prospective clients, with my business card or a short note attached. My photocopy machine makes that a snap.

Multiple-function machines typically combine faxing, copying, and scanning. The advantage of this option is that you have only one machine. The disadvantage is that if the machine breaks and requires service—well, you get the picture.

Ways to Get Help When You Work Alone

Some people work alone by choice and don't need staff members. Others work alone because their companies require it, perhaps because of a tight labor market or as a cost-savings measure. Still others work alone because they are not good at utilizing the resources that are otherwise available to them. But none of those circumstances mean that you don't at least occasionally need help—say, for a special project or seasonal need, or as your business grows.

When office automation enabled us to perform most tasks ourselves, assistants and secretaries became a luxury we could no longer afford or justify paying for—or so we thought or were told. As time goes on, however, it is becoming increasingly evident that we can't grow as businesspeople or entrepreneurs if we don't spend the majority of our time doing what we do best—and letting others do what they do best—so that we are free to do what makes us money, makes us happy, and gets us better results. Finding an assistant may be the answer.

Most businessowners immediately assume that hiring an assistant is a $25,000-per-year expense, which seems daunting when you're just starting out. However, you should consider other options, such as hiring a high-school or college student for a few hours a week, a stay-at-home mom who will work from her home, or a vocational school student who needs the experience for a résumé.

In this age of e-mail, faxes, express mail, high-speed Internet service, and the good old-fashioned telephone,

> We can't grow as businesspeople or entrepreneurs if we don't spend the majority of our time doing what we do best—and letting others do what they do best.

RESOURCES: FOR HOME-BASED BUSINESSES

PUBLICATIONS AND WEB SITES

- *Home Business Magazine* (www .homebusinessmag.com). A Web-based resource site for home-based business owners, home-office workers, and telecommuters. (A subscription to the print version of the magazine is $15 per year for 6 issues.)
- *Better Buys for Business* (www .betterbuys.com; 800-247-2185; $150 for a subscription of ten issues, including any updates; $29 to $39 per single issue, plus $3 for shipping and handling). Annually updated buyers' guides to office equipment, including copiers, fax machines, scanning systems, and printers.
- *Working Solo* (www.workingsolo.com). A monthly e-mail newsletter with news, information, tips, and insights on self-employment.

OFFICE-SUPPORT SERVICES

Office-support services are one of the fastest-growing industries today. You might want to supplement your home office with individual services such as rental of a post-office box, printing and mailing, and hourly rental of equipment such as computers and printers. Or, in lieu of a home office, you could go so far as to rent office space that comes with a package of services, such as answering services, mail rooms, and conference rooms, and puts a variety of equipment at your disposal.

VIRTUAL ASSISTANTS

The International Virtual Assistants Association (17939 Chatsworth St., Suite 102, Los Angeles, CA 91344; 877-440-2750; www.ivaa.org) is the professional association of virtual assistants—independent contractors who provide administrative support or specialized business services at a distance. The association certifies members who pass a five-hour certification exam in the areas of ethics, Internet skills, written communication skills, and office skills. Its Web site allows you to search for a virtual assistant by services, type of software or hardware skills required, country or state. It also offers several online directories that are searchable.

it may not even be necessary to have someone planted in your office for him or her to be useful to you. A new breed of worker, called a virtual assistant, is cropping up all over the country. Virtual assistants offer a broad range of support from a distance, using all of the aforementioned means of communication to work with you, and could become invaluable to you.

Virtual assistants charge $35 to $75 an hour, and you pay only for the time they actually spend working for you. They usually require you to commit to a minimum

FROM MY FILES: VIRTUALLY ME

The Hemphill Productivity Institute team consists of me and my office manager in separate offices in my home (which includes a 15-seat theater for seminars). Virtual team members, all of whom work part-time with me, include a project manager and virtual assistant in Pensacola, a public-relations manager in Orlando, a Web designer and strategist in Atlanta, a writer and editor in Maryland, and a CFO and a COO (both part-time) in Pennsylvania. We communicate by phone and e-mail, meet in person about once or twice a year, and share files and information via the Internet. Thanks to modern technology, all of us can access my databases as necessary.

number of hours per month, but you will be relieved of employment costs, such as insurances and benefits.

To get started, you could hire outsourced services for basic office functions such as bookkeeping, payroll processing, insurance maintenance, and courier service, but there are many more functions that virtual assistants can perform, such as:

- **Database management and data processing**
- **Desktop publishing**
- **Event planning**
- **Graphical presentation**
- **Mail and e-mail services**
- **Marketing**
- **Personnel assistance**
- **Personnel and human resources**
- **Purchasing and supply procurement**
- **Research**
- **Secretarial services**
- **Telephone and fax services**
- **Transcription**
- **Travel planning**
- **Web design and Internet-related services**
- **Writing, editing and proofreading**

A virtual assistant can be a key player in the success of your business, and the more the relationship develops, the more the virtual assistant can help you.

CHAPTER 12

When You Work on the Road

Just because you're on the road doesn't mean that you can't take care of business as usual—if you have the right tools. I often find my travel time to be my most productive because I'm less distracted by phone calls and other interruptions. Because I find new places and things inspiring, travel time is the best time for me to work on projects that require creativity and concentration. And sometimes, being productive while traveling means catching up on some much-needed rest.

A Phone to Go

Most business people have cellular phones. If you use one because you want other people to reach you wherever you are, you'll also need voice-mail service to catch calls that you're not able to answer. You can purchase voice mail from the cellular phone company with your cellular service package or from a separate provider. Your voice-mail message should direct your caller to leave a message or call you at another number. Another option is to forward calls from the cellular phone to another number.

Taking down and sorting messages from a phone while you're working in the car—much less driving in it—is an exercise in self-discipline. It's extremely easy to misplace information and fail to follow up on important items. Whenever possible, listen to messages while the car is parked, so that you can record the messages while you listen. To do this, you can:

- **Write directly into your calendar.**
- **Have a separate loose-leaf notebook** for telephone messages.

If you're good at extracting important information as you listen and you have enough space in your calendar or planner, writing the message there will help prevent you from overlooking it. Because I often write down more information than I need, I make notes on a notepad, and then extract the important information from my notes and write it into my calendar.

Cope With Computers

If computing is essential when you're on the road, a laptop or personal digital assistant is the answer. Be sure to take along a back-up battery, as most batteries won't last long enough for a transcontinental flight—unless you're in business class, where you will have access to an outlet and need an adapter.

Some printers are compact enough to take with you, but if you rarely print, the extra weight isn't justified. You'll probably have access to a printer at your client's office, in your hotel's business center, or at a nearby copy shop (many of which are open 24 hours).

FROM MY FILES: AN IN-CAR OFFICE

For many people, particularly those in sales, the car is their office much of the time, and they need to outfit it accordingly. This necessity presents a unique organizing challenge. A sales representative for a carpet company called me for assistance because he frequently arrived at an appointment only to discover that he had left an important sample or piece of information at home. To solve the problem, he made a list of everything he used during the course of a week. From his list, we created a checklist that he used prior to leaving his office to make sure he had everything he might need in the car. We used large laundry baskets with clearly visible labels to organize the carpet samples by price range. Finally, a portable filebox held all the printed material he needed, and a small plastic caddy held office supplies he frequently needed.

Paying for printing can be prohibitively expensive, so planning ahead to avoid or manage the need for printing is highly recommended.

Record Your Thoughts

While driving, I rely on a small portable tape recorder for dictating ideas, summarizing information that I get from audiotapes, and providing instructions to my assistant about what to do with the information that I've recorded. When my trip is over, I give my assistant the tape to transcribe and take action as indicated.

Keep Track of Your Files

I carry many Action Files with me when I travel—Call, Calls Expected, Discuss With Brooke (my assistant), Read, File—as well as a file for each project that I plan to work on while I'm on the road. I have a briefcase that zips across the top, so that I can easily grab a paper from one of my files while I'm on the run.

Pendaflex (www.Pendaflex.com) sells a portable filing system called the Pendaflex Mobile File, that's essentially a traveling file cabinet the size of a briefcase. File pockets hang vertically when you're in your office—great for small spaces—and fold together with a handle for easy portability.

Work at the Airport

If you've got a cellular phone and a laptop, setting up a mini-office in an airport while waiting for a flight is relatively simple. If you expect to be in the airport for some time, look for an inactive gate for more privacy and quiet in which to think, discuss business, or use the phone.

As use of laptop computers becomes ever more popular, some airports are installing cubicles at the gates, where you can plug in your laptop and work while you wait. You may even have access to high-speed Internet connections for a fee charged to your credit card.

Many frequent travelers join airline clubs to take

FROM MY FILES: GREETINGS

One of my favorite airport activities while waiting for airplanes is shopping for greeting cards. There's always a newsstand near the gate where I can use that 15 minutes before I get on the plane—and it's less fattening than eating an ice cream cone. Often I write personal notes on the plane and mail them at my next stop. If the cards are for a particular event in the future, or if I just want to have one on hand, I put them in the to-file folder that I carry with me when I travel and file them with my other cards when I return to my office.

advantage of the lounges they provide. If you don't have luggage to check, you can get your boarding pass there and make reservation changes. The lounges provide a place to store carry-on luggage, get refreshments, make telephone calls, send faxes, and use your computer and the Internet.

Make sure that you respect your travel companions when using your equipment. Make phone conversations as brief as possible, and remember that they are not private. There's nothing worse than being forced to listen to someone else loudly carry on their business when you're trying to get something done or take a well-deserved nap.

If you're concerned about the privacy of your computer screen, you can purchase a privacy/antiglare filter that allows you to view the screen when you are sitting directly in front of it, but prevents others from seeing it from behind or to the side of you.

Work in Flight

Airline regulations require that you not use portable electronic equipment during take-off and landing. At no time may you use a cellular phone, because of the possibility of its interfering with airplane communication systems.

Many airplanes have telephones in the seatbacks that you can use with your credit card. GTE's AirFone,

> ## TIP: FOR SECURITY'S SAKE
>
> Security is becoming a bigger and more complex issue for business-people who travel. Here are some tips for safeguarding your equipment.
>
> - **If you're traveling by car,** keep as much of your equipment as possible out of sight.
> - **If you're traveling by plane or train** and must pass through security check-points, make sure to keep your laptop in sight at all times.
> - **If you're staying in a hotel,** never leave your computer or other equipment in the room when you're out.
>
> - **Give serious consideration** to the consequences of having equipment stolen—it does happen. What is your "Plan B" for getting your work done? (You might consider taking along a back-up diskette of critical files that you keep in a separate location from your laptop.)
> - **Regardless of how you travel,** be sure to check your insurance policies' limits and deductibles to make sure that your equipment is properly insured, and purchase appropriate riders if necessary.

for example, can be used to transfer data from your laptop while in the air. The system supports computer modems at 9,600 bps (bytes per second), or a minimum of 4,800 bps when there's lots of traffic. It's only a matter of time before you'll be able to enjoy high-speed Internet service while in flight, too.

Work in Your Hotel Room

Hotels have become more business-traveler friendly. When making your hotel reservations check out what facilities and equipment are available in the room and nearby.

Most hotels have business centers on site that can provide virtually any business service that you might need—but usually for a hefty price. Nonetheless, because time is often precious when you are traveling, the cost may be worth it to you. Hotel concierges can also be helpful in locating services that you might need.

After you check in, set up a mini-office in your hotel room. Put the wastebasket next to your desk so that you can throw out excess paper as often as possible. Since

TIP: IMPROVE YOUR PRODUCTIVITY WHILE ON TRAVEL

- **Use your calendar or planner to record telephone messages,** expenses, and mileage (if applicable), as well as your appointments.
- **Keep all receipts together in one place.** A designated pocket in your briefcase or purse would work.
- **Use three-ring binders to neatly hold sales sheets,** order forms, or other paperwork. They're easy to transport and look professional Alternatives: Rubbermaid sells a storage clipboard (14 1/2 x 10 x 3 inches) that holds papers, pens and pencils, and so on, as well as an Autodesk that turns the passenger seat of your car into a desk to hold files, equipment, supplies, and so on.
- **Use a portable file box** (see page 131), available from office-supply stores, to hold papers that you need to use at home and in your mobile office. This will minimize duplication of files between both places.
- **Create Action and Reference Files** in your portable system, so that, as appropriate, you can integrate them back into your system at the office. You may find it helpful to use color to visually separate the two types of files.
- **Be sure to include a to-file folder,** just as you use the to-file box in your office, to identify papers that you need to file when you return to the office. Enclose a copy of your file index for your reference.
- **Make it a habit** to determine at the end of each day which files you will need to return to your office.
- **Use plastic file crates,** available from home or office-supply stores, to organize literature and samples and keep them from sliding all over the car. You can keep them in the trunk or line them up along the backseat, as needed.
- **Create an office-supply caddy** to hold supplies such as a stapler, scissors, paper clips, pens, packing tape and stamps. Organizing stores and catalogs carry various sizes and shapes of caddies, many of them with lids.
- **Keep stationery in the portable file box** to keep it clean and prevent it from getting dog-eared.
- **Use a note pad fastened to the dashboard or windshield** with suction cups for jotting down quick notes.

paper will pile up—probably in an ever-heavier briefcase or other carry-on bag—try to take action at the end of each day.

If you are expecting telephone calls or plan to make calls, check out the phone system. Do you want to record your personal message on the hotel voice-mail

---

TOOL: OFFICE SUPPLIES TO TAKE WITH YOU

- Adhesive notes
- Blank airbills for overnight shipping
- Business cards
- Large mailing envelopes
- Manila folders
- Mini stapler
- Pens, pencils
- Permanent marker for addressing packages
- Pre-addressed labels to mail packages home
- Postage stamps
- Small calculator to figure expense report (unless you use one on your computer or personal digital assistant)
- Stationery for writing quick notes

If you carry a computer:
- Modem, and a connector cable and AC adapter if your modem requires them
- RJ-II phone cord
- Spare batteries
- A data-compression program, such as WinZip, which will allow you to more easily send large files as e-mail attachments
- Blank floppy disks in case you need to transfer data by means other than e-mail
- A list of local phone numbers for dialing up your Internet provider wherever you will be

If you're traveling overseas:
- Electrical and phone adapters as needed
- Passport and necessary visas
- Travelers checks, local currency

---

system? Does your room have call waiting or two lines so that you don't miss an important call? If you're planning to make calls on the hotel phone, be sure to check out the rate card—even for local calls. If you're making lots of calls, you may want to use your cell phone or the pay phone in the lobby. To avoid the outrageous long-distance rates that many hotels charge, it's always a good idea to carry a prepaid phone card or a long-distance calling card.

You also need to be prepared to take messages. Instead of scribbling on the nearest piece of paper, I record messages in my Planner Pad or the spiral notebook that I carry in my briefcase. This technique eliminates excess paper and lost messages.

For more on staying organized and handling all the various kinds of the paperwork you accumulate while traveling for business, see the next chapter, "When You

Attend a Convention." There is probably no better example of potential for paperwork chaos and overburdenig than when you attend a convention. The strategies outlined in that discussion will serve you well on any business trip.

CHAPTER 13

When You Attend a Convention

You know how it happens: You walk around the exhibit hall and pick up samples, brochures, business cards, order forms. You attend seminars and make notes, get handouts—and more business cards. You return to your hotel room and retrieve voice-mail messages from your room phone and your office phone, e-mail messages on your computer, and faxes under your door. And, of course, you gather receipts.

You return home with every intention of organizing all the material, but a stack of paper that accumulated while you were away greets you. It looks more threatening than the bags you brought home from the convention. So you stack the stuff from the convention on a shelf in your office, planning to get to it later. After several weeks, you're tired of looking at the stack, so you put the papers in a file labeled something like "Association Meeting—Chicago—2002," which is probably in front of the one you labeled similarly for 2001. Of course, you never look at the material again.

Make a Plan Before You Go

Read the material provided by the meeting planner, and decide which seminars and events you want to attend. If you can't attend a session but want the information, you may be able to get an audiotape.

Make a list of your objectives for attending the meeting and rank them in order of importance. Use your calendar to schedule your time, writing in pencil so

As you attend the meetings, carry one file folder labeled "Act" and another labeled "File."

that you can make any changes as necessary. One convention attendee told me that, to help her keep to her schedule, she organized her purchase orders in order as she planned to visit booths.

If other people from your organization will be going, use the "divide and conquer" technique. Plan your schedules together to get the most results for your time and money.

If making contact with someone specific is a high priority, begin making plans before you go. For example, call and invite the person to have breakfast with you.

If you're combining business and pleasure on this trip and are bringing along family members, make sure they know what to expect: what to wear, when they can expect to attend functions with you, and when they'll be on their own. Make childcare arrangements before you arrive.

Be prepared to create an office in your hotel room. Pack some office supplies, and be sure to take a notebook or use a section of your calendar, so that all the notes you write during the event will be in one place.

Attending a convention can be exhausting. By all means make sure that you'll be as physically comfortable as possible:

- **Be prepared for convention** and hotel rooms that are often cold.
- **Don't buy new shoes for the event.** This is not a good time to break them in.
- **If you expect to pick up lots of catalogs** or other heavy items, a backpack or a carry-on bag with wheels may come in very handy. You could even attach a pre-addressed box with bungee cords to a fold-up luggage carrier; when you're done with the convention, you can easily ship your box of materials back home.
- **A fanny pack is great for business cards,** your hotel room key, a credit card, or other small items.

Stay Organized Throughout

Once you get to the convention, you're ready to take advantage of your advance planning. Keep the materials that you collect organized as you go, and the convention—and the days afterward—will be much more pleasant and productive.

Paper

Start by setting up a mini-office in your hotel. As you attend the meetings, carry one file folder labeled "Act" and another labeled "File." Remember that every piece of paper you collect will require one of three actions: File, Act, or Toss. Every time you go by a wastebasket, check to see if you're carrying something that you should toss in there!

Many of the pieces of paper that you collect at the convention will not require immediate action, but do contain information that might be useful in the future. These items go in your to-file folder. Ask yourself the familiar question: If I want this information again, what word will I think of first? Write your answer on the item's upper right-hand corner. If you already have a File Index, take it with you to the convention, so that you avoid creating a file for "Résumés" when you already have one for "Bios." If you don't have a File Index, this is an excellent opportunity to start one.

The remaining pieces of paper require your action. Ask yourself: What is the next action I want to take on this piece of paper? Write the answer in the upper right-hand corner, and then when you have some time at a break or back in your hotel room, decide how you'll handle that action. If you have someone to whom you can delegate the task, create a file for that person and put the paper there. If you need to take the action by a certain day, put a reminder in your calendar.

Catalogs

As you review catalogs that you've collected, note on the front covers any items of interest so that you don't have go back through them again.

Things to Ship Home

Use preprinted address labels to ship back items that are too heavy to carry home in your luggage. If you're going to be away for several days and you have an assistant

Every time you go by a wastebasket, check to see if you're carrying something that you should toss in there!

TIP: ORGANIZING BUSINESS CARDS

- **Make sure you use one pocket** of your jacket, wallet, or briefcase for your cards and another for other people's cards.
- **On each card,** note the date and place you got it.
- **Don't hesitate** to throw away cards from people whom you know you won't ever contact.
- **If no action is required** and you or someone else will enter the cards in a card file or computer program, identify the key retrieval word by asking yourself: If I wanted to contact this person again, what word would I think of first? Put the cards all together in one place—a briefcase pocket or an envelope in an Action File for computer entry. Here's where technology shines. A business-card scanner combined with a contact-manager program will make this task much easier.

- **If you want to take an action,** put it in the appropriate Action File. For example, if you want to call for an appointment, make a note in your calendar on the day you plan to make the call, and file the business card in your call folder—or toss it in the wastebasket if you recorded elsewhere all the information that you need.
- **If you've met someone and want to send follow-up material** that you don't have with you, make a note on the person's business card and put in the appropriate Action File, such as Call, Discuss With, or Data Entry.
- **If you ever use your own business card** to write notes to yourself, make sure to put an "x" on the front of the card, so that you don't accidentally give the card away.

back at the office, ship by overnight service any papers that he or she can handle while you're away.

Expense Receipts and Reports

Put all expense receipts in one place, such as an envelope in your briefcase. I put the receipts in my wallet when I pay the bill or make the purchase, and at the end of the day, transfer them all to my receipt envelope. Include copies of your expense-reimbursement forms. It's easier to record the purpose of an expense when you incur it than it is to reconstruct it later.

Thank-You Notes

Write quick thank-you notes as you go. A less-than-perfect thank you is better than no thank you at all. In your calendar, keep a list of the notes you have written so you won't forget someone important or write duplicates.

Stay Focused

Refer to your list of objectives frequently to be sure that you're on target. But don't hesitate to make changes if the situation warrants it.

Follow Up When You Get Home

When you're in the midst of something, it's easy to say, "Next time I will_____." But unless you make a note of it now, the idea will be long forgotten when your convention rolls around again next year. If you plan to attend this convention or a similar one again next year, write an "After Convention Report" to use as a guide for next year: What worked well for you? What you would do differently? Why?

If you follow these suggestions, you'll return to your office having to face only one pile of the paper—the one that accumulated there while you were gone. But more importantly, those papers you collected on your trip will be a real resource, and not just another pile of postponed decisions.

CHAPTER 14

When Your Space Is Shared or Downsized

I n today's world of work, employees and professionals often find themselves working in nontraditional work environments. Here are some tips for staying organized when working in the most common of these new work environments.

Moving Into a Workstation

G iven a choice, most people would prefer to have a traditional office rather than a workstation, also known as a cubicle or modular office. But many organizations are trying to put more people in less space, and workstations are the result. Given the fact that clutter expands to the space available for its retention, workstations can have a positive effect by forcing people to purge unnecessary information. Still, for the person who needs to keep a whole library of books or other materials on hand, a workstation can pose a real challenge.

Although workstations may seem to be designed to be one-size-fits-all, which is a cost-effective option for the employer, virtually all workstations can be designed to take into account workers' various needs and workstyles, and more creative options are becoming available as the market demands them. One woman who moved into a new workstation discovered that the computer dominated the corner desk area, the only part of the workstation that could function as a traditional desk, since it was centrally located with a kneehole area and recessed lighting. Recognizing that she spent as much time working on the telephone as on the computer, and

TIP: FOR ODD COUPLES

One of the toughest assignments occurs when people with highly organized workstyles and those with very casual workstyles are thrown together into an office. Here are the keys to success in that situation:

- **Sensitivity.** Each person must recognize that he or she is not *right* and the other person is not *wrong.* An overzealous neatnik can be just as irritating as a perennial slob!

- **Boundaries.** The very casual half of the duo needs to confine his or her creativity to specific areas within the office.

- **Acknowledgment.** Each person needs to acknowledge the other's strengths and his or her own weaknesses.

wanting space to spread her work out and read the newspapers that her job required her to read, she moved the computer to one side and set up her desk in the corner. The moral here is, don't assume that you can't adapt a workstation to your needs.

The truth is that when we have plenty of space we don't always organize most efficiently the things we use. A client of mine moved into her new workspace. As she needed things, she took them from boxes and put them on and in her desk. After a month, she discovered, much to her amazement, that she never used most of what she had carted from her last office.

Probably the most difficult adjustment from a private office to a shared or more open workspace is learning to live with the lack of privacy in conversation. Learning to speak more quietly on the telephone—and off—will require vigilance and sensitivity. For certain phone calls, you may want to find an empty conference room with a door that you can shut.

Many of the space and storage issues that arise when a workplace converts to workstations are addressed in Part Four, Reorganizing the Organization. However, just prior to moving into workstations might be a great time to:

- **Establish a company-wide File Clean-Out Day** (see Chapter 16).
- **Set up a department-wide supply closet.**

- **Plan a department-wide library** to which everyone can contribute books and other materials. (Of course, the success of this idea presumes that you can also assign someone to keep that library organized.)
- **Assess the need for off-site storage** of archival materials or Reference Files.

Space for the Day

In companies that employ many telecommuters, office spaces are available to whomever needs one on a given day, a practice referred to as "hoteling." Other professionals may work at a client site occasionally or temporarily and are given access to a desk, chair, and telephone, and perhaps a computer. In either situation, you must come prepared to set up shop quickly and close it up and take it away quickly—posing challenges similar to working from your car or traveling for business. In Chapters 12 and 13, you'll find plenty of helpful tips that apply to this situation.

When you arrive at the worksite, be sure to check in with the receptionist or whomever can help ensure that anyone who needs to find you during the day can do so. You don't want to miss telephone calls or meetings because your name isn't recognized or you're hidden away in a cubicle and no one knows where you are.

When You Share an Office

Sharing an office has become more and more of a reality in many organizations—an unfortunate one, in my opinion. Because of differing workstyles, sharing space poses one of the biggest and touchiest organizing challenges. Instead of sharing as a solution to overcrowding, it would be better to create more and smaller spaces.

However, if you must regularly share an office—and even more difficult, a desk—with someone, communication and common courtesy will be the keys to success, particularly if you also need to share information and action.

> **When you arrive at the worksite, be sure to check in with the receptionist or whomever can help ensure that anyone who needs to find you during the day can do so.**

Here are just some of the issues that you and your officemate may need to discuss:

- **Will we share office supplies?** For shared supplies, set up a supply checklist, and make the person who uses the last one of something responsible for replenishing the supply (see the discussion of organizing storage closets, on page 27). You may not want to share everything, so find a place where you can keep those items that you wish your officemate to honor as off-limits.

- **If we're sharing space but using it at different hours, how should we set it up?** Identify specific drawers for each user if at all possible.

- **Should we clean off the desk at the end of our shifts?** Even if cleaning up your stuff isn't absolutely necessary, it is highly desirable in these circumstances.

- **Will we alternate use of the same chair?** If you can't get your own desk chairs, at least try to get one chair that allows you to easily change its height and other settings. Otherwise, you may find yourselves fighting with the chair at the beginning of your shifts or working in an ill-fitting chair, which could eventually wreak havoc with your productivity.

- **How will we hand off work in progress, so that we each know where the other left off?** You will need a separate container—a tray, hanging file, hot file, or drawer—to contain materials that are in progress. Be sure to attach notes to those materials to indicate their status. It may also be valuable to create a status report at the end of each shift.

- **How will we handle messages for each other?** You'll need to agree on the best way to give messages to each other. In my office, we have a spiral-bound book for all incoming messages. In this way, we can each see what has come in and what has been completed.

PART 4

Reorganizing the Organization

CHAPTER 15

Assess Your System

An association once hired me to work with an employee whom it was about to fire. At the last minute, the association president had had second thoughts and called me to evaluate the situation. I discovered that the employee in question was demoralized, poorly trained, and working for three bright, but very disorganized managers, all of whom were saddled with a disastrous filing system that didn't serve any of them.

I provided organizing-skills training for the employee and the managers, and together we designed and implemented an effective filing system for the department.

The result was a productive assistant who enjoyed her job, three managers who felt they had adequate staff support and information when they needed it—and file drawers that were 50% empty!

Just as in this case, in my more than 20 years as a consultant to individuals and businesses, I've discovered that many people are disorganized because their working environment—their company or their department—is disorganized. Early in my career I often worked with people who were trying to make the best of a bad situation. Now I know that if the organization is not organized, it is virtually impossible for its workers to be successfully organized in the long run. That's why, if you're running a business or are charged with improving the efficiency, cost-effectiveness, and productivity of all or part of your organization, you'll want to pay special attention to this section of *Taming the Paper Tiger at Work.*

How Management Contributes to the Problem

One of the challenges of organizing an organization is that top management doesn't want to be bothered with it. In fact, the time it takes to say "file it" may be all the time senior management devotes to records management. This poses a serious problem.

If you're a member of top management and you're reading this, then you know you've got a problem and you're probably getting ready to do something about it. If you're not a member of top management, then you may want to bring the problem to management's attention.

I once worked with a law firm whose files were seriously overcrowded. An obvious solution was to convert traditional drawer filing to movable open-shelf filing, which holds more records in less space. In the process of transferring the files from drawers to the new units, I discovered huge files with excessive duplication. Many files could have been reduced 75% simply by purging and eliminating the duplicates. Some files were more than 25 years old.

When I told my client, he said his time was too valuable to spend purging files. When I suggested that he hire a law student, who could exercise some informed judgment about what to throw out, he responded, "Nobody can remove anything from the files except me." He felt he was too important to do the job himself, but no one else was important enough. So his files continued to grow—and so did his original problem.

FROM MY FILES: WASTED TIME

From a survey of 200 executives of large companies commissioned by Accountemps Inc., executives waste 10.7% of their total work time because they or their assistants can't find something. Assuming a 40-hour workweek, that's the equivalent of 5 ½ workweeks wasted over one year.

The Solution

As we discussed earlier in this book, organizing in and of itself has no intrinsic value. Highly organized businesses have gone bankrupt. Highly organized employees have lost their jobs. Organization is not the key to success—knowing what is important is. But organizing will help a company meet its goals, ultimately with less money, time, and effort. It's a form of the old chicken-and-egg question: I've worked with organizations that weren't clear about what information was important, but organizing it—beginning with eliminating what they know is not important—helped them decide what was important.

The techniques I'm going to describe aren't complicated, but they do take time. As a result, they're often neglected until the tiger strikes—say, when the auditors appear or a key person falls ill—and the results can be costly. This part of the book is about what steps you—as a self-employed person, business owner,

FROM MY FILES: TWO CASES

She Left With the Goods

The receptionist in a hair salon left after 17 years. Although she was the lowest-paid employee in the company, her bosses quickly discovered that the information she had accumulated about the day-to-day workings of the business was invaluable. She was the one who knew which vendor was the most reliable, which catalog had the special product that a long-time client ordered every six months, and whom to call if the soda machine wouldn't give back change. Unfortunately, she had gathered the information in her head and took it with her when she left.

The Opportunity Cost of Chaos

The manager of a mortgage company wanted to hire a new loan officer, but he couldn't persuade the person he wanted to join the company. Several months later, while talking with the prospective employee, the manager was shocked to discover why. "I decided not to join your company because of the way the office looked," the fellow said. "I felt it looked out of control, and I was afraid to join the fray." The manager decided that if his office looked that way to a prospective employee, it must also look that way to a prospective customer— and he hired a professional organizer.

A company's filing system— paper or electronic—can be an indicator of the company's overall health and the clarity of its purpose.

executive, department manager, or supervisor—can take now to minimize the danger of the paper tiger in your organization later. The result will be more than an insurance policy, for you will increase productivity and profit immediately.

Why Paper Is the Starting Point

Perhaps our excitement about the possibilities of technology caused many companies to ignore or neglect paper-records management. Yet surveys show that much of our important information is still maintained on paper. That's why the paper-filing system is the best place in which to begin organizing a company's information. Besides, much of the information stored there can probably be thrown away or put in archives, a move that is psychologically encouraging and motivates people to organize their own files.

As you begin, keep in mind that this isn't a short sprint—it's a long-distance run. Years of accumulation and postponed decisions won't disappear quickly. No one who has designed or improved a filing system would argue that it's a fast or easy task. But businesses today cannot afford to ignore that their continued success—or even survival—will be based on team effectiveness. And effective organization increases team effectiveness. Valuable time is wasted when employees duplicate each other's work; when they produce, copy, or circulate reports or messages that aren't important to every recipient; or when they spend time looking for information that's buried on a desk or in a computer.

A filing system can be an indicator of the company's overall health: It often reflects the power structure, political atmosphere, communication strengths and weaknesses, and clarity of purpose within the organization. If, for example, the files are full of information that is used to prove a certain transaction occurred, it may mean that customer service is weak; instead of responding to the customer's complaint about not receiving a product, em-

FROM MY FILES: THE PAPERLESS OFFICE?

In the mid 1970s futurists held high hopes for the "paperless office," a catch phrase that implied a clutter-free and organized workplace. However, all the current statistics point to the fact that much of the business world is still drowning in the stuff. Consider these: Office-paper consumption in the U.S. increased by 12% from 1995 to 2000, while PC use at work increased by 5%, according to *Time* magazine. According to a study by Xerox, offices in 2005 will use 50% more paper than they did in 1995.

Over the past 15 years or so, the majority of corporate budgets for information management have been spent to acquire technology, and the results, in terms of productivity and the ability of organizations to function effectively and their employees to find the vital information, have been less than stellar. Certainly few people today would be willing to go back to doing manually what we have been doing electronically, but we are faced with new decisions about taming the paper tiger. Now, in addition to organizing paper, we have to organize

our technology. Who hasn't sat in front of a computer screen scrolling up and down, going from window to window, searching for a document that's in there somewhere. Who hasn't agonized over whether to keep that vital information in the computer, or on hard copy, or both? The result? Uncontrolled information that's a burden, not a resource.

Based on my experience, what we really need to do is spend more time teaching people how to make decisions about what information is valuable to keep. Then we can decide which form to keep it in, either paper or electronic.

Besides, in the short term, paper is highly desirable because it is often more user-friendly than reading information off a computer screen, a point made by the experience of a company that banned paper from its offices only to discover that its employees were storing it in their cars.

A great resource recently published on this topic is *The Myth of the Paperless Office,* by Abigail J. Sellers and Richard H.R. Harper (from The MIT Press, 2002).

ployees spend time documenting what went wrong and whose fault it was. Unfortunately, many companies don't recognize this, or if they do, they fail to do anything about it, until it's too late.

A filing system is like the foundation of a building. People may not see it, and it's not as exciting as the building's architecture or its interior decoration, but if you fail to build the foundation well, eventually the building will weaken and fall.

Identify Your Information Resources

█ can ask any manager, "What are your human resources?" and I'll get an organization chart. I can ask, "What are your financial resources?" and I'll get a budget. But if I ask, "What are your information resources?" I get a blank stare.

Stop and think about it. Every business, from a widget manufacturer to a doctor's office, depends on shared information. Human resources come and go, and financial resources change. But everyone has, wants, or needs information, and that information must continue to flow in an organized way, despite changes in the workplace, or the business will suffer and eventually fail. An absence, expected or unexpected, due to restructuring, accident, or illness, makes it essential for management and support staff to work together to develop a system that both groups can use and understand.

In most businesses, few decisions are made about how to structure the system, or how to allow for or control growth. Before long, what was intended to be a re-

TOOL: MANAGEMENT OF INFORMATION RESOURCES

Use the following list of questions to survey the state of information resources in your organization.

- **Is someone responsible** for the information-resource management in your organization or department?
- **Are you confident** that your department or organization retains information as required by law?
- **Have you identified information** that should be retained in an archive as a permanent record?
- **Have you coordinated your paper-filing system** with your computer-

filing system—that is, have you determined when it's appropriate to store something in paper or electronic form or, in some cases, both?

- **Do staff members spend** an appropriate amount of time filing and retrieving information?
- **Are you and others in your department** or organization confident that you can find a piece of paper or a computer document again after it has been given to someone else to file?
- **Does the organization's filing**

source becomes a burden. One person thinks the information should be filed under "Cars," another thinks it's "Automobiles," and still another thinks it's "Vehicles." It becomes difficult to find anything. Before long, information that's important stays in the offices and on the desks of individual employees. The central filing system becomes a dumping ground for paper that probably could have gone in the wastebasket. Now, anyone who wants to find something must roam from office to office or send out a desperate e-mail message asking, "Has anyone seen…?"

A similar situation has evolved with computers. At the onset of the computer age we had a mainframe filing system that demanded that people enter data in a uniform way, just as we used to have Mabel in Central Files to organize the paper filing system. Now, however, many companies teeter on the edge of an information-management disaster because countless of their personal computers have been "organized" by employees who are no more knowledgeable about organizing computer files than they were about organizing paper files.

So, what's the state of your organization's informa-

cabinets and computer system have plenty of room to file new information?

- **Are all cabinets labeled** on the outside to identify the contents?

- **Are all computer diskettes labeled?** Are the labels easy to read and are the diskettes well-filed so that anyone can find them when they need them?

- **Do you schedule time** for you and your staff to regularly purge unnecessary information from your file cabinets and computers?

- **Are filing cabinets,** shelves, and storage rooms free of unidentified piles of paper and diskettes?

- **Does your organization educate** all of its new employees about the filing system?

- **Can a temporary employee** find information in the files when necessary?

- **Would you be comfortable** if your most important client saw how your filing system works?

- **Is your crucial information backed up** in such a way that it could be recovered in the case of an internal or external disaster?

TIP: A NOTE ABOUT SHREDDING

Walk around your office and pull pieces of paper out of the trash and recycling bins. Does the nature of what you find make you uncomfortable? Do the papers contain proprietary information about your company or your clients that you wouldn't want competitors to find? If so, consider shredding. Some clients may contractually require that you provide this precaution. And you may find that having a secure means of eliminating confidential material will eliminate a stumbling block to more effectively eliminating unnecessary paper.

You could hire the services of a shredding company, which may have a mobile unit or will remove paper from your site and handle it in a secure manner. If you decide to purchase your own shredder, make sure you buy high-quality equipment and arrange for ongoing maintenance.

tion resources? Have you clearly identified to all employees what information you need to do business? What resources do they include—in your filing cabinets, computers, bookshelves, and in or on people's desks? How are they organized? How accessible are they to everyone who needs them? How fail-safe is your system for managing these resources? What happens if an employee leaves or you have a major disaster such as a fire or an earthquake?

Use the accompanying list of questions to help you take stock of your organization's information resources. If you're not pleased with what you discover, keep reading.

Prepare for Success

Most people aren't thrilled when they hear, "We're going to organize the office." And with good reason. Frequently, one or more employees have made attempts to reorganize the filing system, straighten the library or clean up the supply room, often resulting in confusion and failure.

You will surely hear protests, such as "My files are personal," and stories, such as the one about a lawsuit won because of boxes of old company files squirreled away in a retiree's garage.

Although records-management programs often meet with initial resistance, it may be minimized if you reassure employees that their records won't be lost or made inaccessible. Employees must also be made aware that all files pertaining to the company belong to the organization. In addition, you should:

Lead by Example

Lead by example and organize your own area before making any announcements.

Promote It

Point out the value and purpose of such a program. You might suggest that your organization will succeed in:
- **Getting rid of clutter.**
- **Spending less time** looking for misfiled information.
- **Simplifying the process** of deciding what to keep and for how long.
- **Eliminating the need to explain** what happened to missing documents in case of a lawsuit.

Communicate Your Goals

Communicate effectively the goals you hope to accomplish. They might include:
- **Eliminating duplication of resources** wherever you possibly can.
- **Making information easily accessible** to everyone who has need of it.
- **Identifying vital records** and ensuring their safety in case of a disaster.
- **Establishing easy-to-use guidelines** for how long everything should be kept.
- **Increasing space** by storing inactive but important records out of the way or elsewhere.
- **Coordinating the information** kept in hard-copy versus in the computer system.

Assign the Responsibility

I've always found it interesting that companies have specialists on staff who are responsible for the computer system. (Although I've also noted that, in many cases,

> ## TIP: TIME FOR CLEAN UP
>
> - **To find an organizer in your area** to help you organize your office, call the National Association of Professional Organizers (NAPO, 1033 La Posada, Suite 220, Austin, TX 78752; 512-206-0151; www.napo.net).
> - **To find a Paper Tiger–authorized consultant** who is trained in my organizing techniques and in how to install the *Paper Tiger* software, visit my Website at www.thepapertiger.com.

the system manager does little to train people about organization and management of computer files.) Why shouldn't they have specialists in a similar position for non-electronic information? In very large companies, it might be a full-time position, referred to as Information Resource Manager or Filing System Manager. In smaller companies it could be part of someone's job or a part-time position.

The position could include these responsibilities:

- **Identifying,** implementing, and maintaining records-retention policies.
- **Analyzing** existing filing systems and reorganizing them when appropriate.
- **Coordinating** storage of hard copy and computer files.
- **Organizing** an annual File Clean-Out Day (discussed in Chapter 16).
- **Training** new employees about the information resources in the company.

Choose this person carefully. Find the most organized person in your office, as well as someone who:

- **Has good rapport** with all kinds of people.
- **Is willing to look for answers** if they need to.
- **Is good with details.**
- **Can handle criticism.**
- **Is willing and able** to design and execute a plan.

Make certain that you state your objectives clearly to your designee, that he or she understands them, and that you have a method to measure success.

You may find it necessary to hire an outside consultant to organize the office initially, and that person can train a staff member to maintain the system. My most exciting projects recently have involved companies that have hired us to develop and implement The Productivity Quickstart™. This program includes training in-house Paper Tiger Administrators who work with the information-systems department to create, coordinate, and implement systems to track and share intellectual information and resources—including everything from paper and electronic media to photographs and office supplies.

Conduct a Records Inventory

The next step is to inventory your existing records and files, department by department. On a preliminary walk-through, sketch all the offices where records are stored. Use an office blueprint if one is available. List the locations (which offices) and types of equipment (legal or letter files, computers, storage cabinets, bookshelves, and so on).

Two people can inventory files more easily than one can. One person reads the names of the files, and the other person notes it, either in a word-processing file or on a notepad. A laptop computer would be ideal for this purpose. If one of the participants is the employee who uses the files, this preliminary exercise will probably result in some files ending up in the trash—where they should have been long ago. By simply looking at files, you may come across ones that are antiquated and disposable. At the very least, the person doing the inventory should ask the files' regular users for recommendations of files that are no longer used. While this step might seem premature, it will allow you to avoid having to waste time and money taking an inventory of something that you will ultimately toss anyway. In my consulting business, if participants are excited about the opportunity to dispose of stuff right away, I start there. If not, then we inventory first and demonstrate how much old stuff there is by providing the dates of those files if they're available.

Records inventory is a big job and may take a long

> **If one of the participants is the employee who uses the files, inventorying files will probably result in some of them ending up in the trash—where they should have been long ago.**

TOOL: KEY QUESTIONS FOR A RECORDS INVENTORY

To make sure that you get consistent information from your records inventory, design a form that includes such information as:

- **Name of the organization**
- **Name of the department** or division
- **Location of the file** (for example, fifth-floor supply room)
- **Type of file storage** (for example, cabinet—vertical or lateral, desk drawer or book shelf)
- **Filing method used**, whether alphabetic, numeric, or other
- **Name of the file category** (for example, Accounting or Personnel)
- **Specific file names**, according to the file labels on top of the manila folders
- **Contents of the file category** in generic terms, if that's not clear from the file's label

time. It's risky to allow employees to conduct their own inventories without the assistance of someone who will be involved in the entire process. Aside from being hard-pressed to find time to do it, employees may provide inconsistent or incomplete information.

CHAPTER 16

Set Up a File Clean-Out Day

A re there items in your office you'd eliminate if you had the time to do so? Sure there are. And, no doubt, that's true for every person in your office.

A File Clean-Out Day endorsed by management sends the message that managing paper effectively is an essential part of day-to-day business, not to be relegated to "some Saturday." Depending on the nature of your business, you may need to schedule a File Clean-Out Day for all departments on the same day or for different ones on different days.

One CEO of an 80-employee company summed up the imperative pretty well: After spending a day cleaning up his own office, the CEO called everyone together for my "Taming the Paper Tiger" seminar. He introduced it by saying, "Here is a list of the crucial things you need to keep. The rest of it you don't need. You are not going to get larger cubicles, so start tossing."

If your organization hasn't systematically cleaned out its files for several years, dedicating just one day to the task will probably not be enough, but it is a good place to start.

Here's how to organize your big day:

Carefully select the day. Choose a time when business demands are least. Many organizations find it practical to use the same day each year. One company holds an "Annual St. Patrick's Day Clean-Out" while another calls it "Dump Day." One former client has two days per year, in April and in October: Fool's Day and Ghoul's Day.

TIP: WHAT'S LOST IS FOUND

File Clean-Out Day is also a good opportunity to locate missing documents or other items of importance. For example, one organization was missing some back issues of its newsletter that it wanted to keep for posterity. By alerting staff members to this need, the organization recovered all of the missing copies during its File Clean-Out Day.

Announce the day well in advance, and designate specific hours for beginning and ending it. Make certain that everyone understands that they are expected to participate; no one is too important, too unimportant, or too busy. It's essential that members of management actively participate and demonstrate their support of the project. With some clients I've done a "pilot project" with the head of a department to determine whether the results would be worth the investment. In those cases, the client has served as a role model for the rest of the staff.

Plan a separate clean-out day for your computer files. Computer files also need to be purged—but not on the same day as your paper files. Not only will you not have enough time for both tasks, but it's also difficult to work with both mediums simultaneously. However, the process is the same as I've described for paper files. (For more on the nuts and bolts organizing computer files, see Chapter 9.)

As one company I know does, you could simultaneously schedule routine computer maintenance with File Clean-Out Day. Once the computer system is down for maintenance, no one can bury him- or herself in work on the computer instead of in the paper files.

Assign one person as coordinator of File Clean-Out Day. Choose someone who has good rapport with the staff, is good with details, and has read this book. Ideally, it should be the person who has also been or will be assigned as information-resource manager or filing-system manager.

Work with the coordinator to develop or provide materials to support the day. These might include:

- A copy of any existing Retention Guidelines (see Chapter 17)
- A "What to do if…" tipsheet (see the following page)
- Guidelines for an effective File Clean-Out Day (see pages 166–167).

Hire temporary employees to answer the telephones. If there are specific calls that staff members must receive, instruct them to notify the temps to send the calls through.

Provide large trash receptacles, extra recycling boxes, trash bags, marking pens and labels. One company had fluorescent orange labels printed with "Basura"—trash in Spanish—because the cleaning crew did not read English. Identify a specific place where staff members can leave reusable supplies and equipment for recycling by others who might need them.

Notify the building maintenance crew that there will be extra trash on that day. Engage their cooperation, as needed, to move heavy boxes, trash barrels, and so on. It may be helpful to offer a cash bonus.

Encourage everyone to maximize their energy. Cleaning files is physically—and mentally—tiring. Staff members should be as physically comfortable as possible. Set an example by following these steps yourself:

- Wear comfortable shoes.
- Sit in a chair in front of the file drawers, or bring groups of files to your desk.
- Use good lifting techniques to avoid back strain.
- Throw trash into a smaller wastebasket and then empty that into a larger bin or recycling box to avoid having to lift overly heavy burdens.

Encourage staff to label file cabinets or groups of files with adhesive notes that indicate what further action is

> Once the computer system is down for routine maintenance, no one can bury him- or herself in work on the computer instead of in the paper files.

TOOL: THE "WHAT DO IF" TIPSHEET

This handout should describe the nuts-and-bolts procedures for File Clean-Out Day, such as where to get supplies and whom to contact if there's a problem. For example:

If you need:
File folders, labels, tape, etc., get them from _____

File boxes and file-box labels (to send materials off-site), get them from

_____

Physical help to move boxes, contact

_____

What if you:
Have materials that need to be taken to the file-storage room? Only materials that have been thoroughly inventoried and clearly labeled can be taken to storage. To have the items picked up, call

_____

Have materials that need to be saved but are rarely accessed? These materials can be sent to off-site storage. Materials must be thoroughly inventoried and clearly labeled. Off-site storage costs will be paid by _____

_____

To get further information, call _____

_____

Find materials that belong in another area? Place the items in a box and clearly label the contents and desired destination. Be careful not to mix boxes that are to be saved with boxes of trash.

Find materials that aren't listed on the Retention Guidelines, but you think should be kept? Mention the item on your Problem Identification Form. Leave the items in your files until the issue is resolved. If you have questions, ask

_____

About phone coverage
The reception desk will answer all telephones. If you must take a call, leave notice with the reception desk.

About trash removal
Several locations have been designated for depositing trash, which will be picked up by the cleaning crew. You may leave trash at your own workstation if it is labeled with a trash sticker, available from _____

_____

_____

Use the usual recycling bins for materials other than paper.

Don't throw away file folders that are still in good condition. Reuse them whenever you can or take them to the designated area in the supply room.

TIP: ARCHIVING

If you have plenty of space, you don't need archives. Archives are created when you need space to store files you don't necessarily use but do need to keep. See Chapters 2 and 17 for more on for Retention Guidelines.

required. The notes might direct, for example, "Discuss with…," "Move to…," "Type labels," and so on. During the group meeting at the end of the day, a record of the notes may provide clues to deciding how to move ahead with the project. The next step might include scheduling another clean-out day for everyone or continuing the process individually.

Be creative. Bring a camera for before-and-after photos that can be posted on bulletin boards or printed in the company newsletter. Consider awards for the oldest, funniest, strangest, or other kind of item. (Here's a true example: One office found the back half of a donkey pinata. What could they have been saving that for?) Some of my clients have ordered T-shirts with an appropriate theme for the occasion—another way to increase participants' comfort.

Let staff members keep their choice of stuff that would otherwise have been thrown out, such as notebooks or reference materials.

Serve a simple, but good quality lunch for everyone. This will encourage communication between staff members about decisions they've made and what remains to be done and enables them to return to their tasks as soon as possible. It also promotes camaraderie—they will all have a story to share about their experiences.

Gather together all staff members 30 minutes before the designated ending time. Genuinely thank everyone for contributing to this important effort. Ask them to answer the following questions on an evaluation form:

Continued on page 168

TIP: SIX STEPS TO AN EFFECTIVE FILE CLEAN-OUT DAY

Here is a quick reminder on how to use File Clean-Out Day most effectively. *(Note:* Much of this advice is discussed in more detail in Part One of this book. I've occasionally cross-referenced the step to an appropriate, earlier chapter.)

Step 1: What do I need to keep?

Before choosing to keep any file or piece of paper, ask the Art of Wastebasketry questions (described in Chapter 2):

- Does this information require my action?
- Does it exist elsewhere?
- Is this information recent enough to be useful?
- Can I identify how I would use it?
- Are there tax or legal implications to keeping or disposing of this?
- What is the worst possible thing that would happen if I didn't have this piece of paper?

Step 2: Where do I keep it?

If you choose to keep the paper or the file, put it in one of the following major categories (see Chapters 3, 4, and 8):

- Action files, which you should store in or on your desk or in a cabinet or shelf near your desk.
- Current Reference Files, which are used or could be used for current projects and should also be easily accessible from your desk.
- Outdated reference (historical or archival) files, which aren't necessary for current projects, but are desirable

or necessary to keep for historical or legal reasons. These needn't be readily accessible.

Step 3: How do I keep it? (see Chapter 3)

- Use hanging files whenever possible. If you expect to remove only a piece of paper at the time from the file, no manila file is necessary inside the hanging file. If you expect to take out the hanging file's entire contents, use a manila file inside.
- If manila files are used for subdivisions within a hanging file, label each manila file with its larger category and subtitle. When hanging files become thick, use box-bottom files.
- Use color only if it tells a story (for example, all Administrative Files are red, and all program files are green).
- Replace paper clips with staples or the smallest possible binder clip.
- Stamp or write "FILE COPY: DO NOT REMOVE" on any item when applicable. Enclose the original copy of a form or anything used for making additional copies in a plastic sheet protector.
- Be certain that all papers have a date, and file them in chronological order with the most recent item at the front of the file.
- When using plastic tabs, choose clear or light colored ones for ease of reading. Place plastic tabs on the front of hanging files. Stagger the tabs across the tops of the hanging

files so that all of the labels will be visible when the drawer is opened.

- When labeling a manila file, place the file name as close to the top of the tab as possible. If you're using colored labels, you can minimize the possibility of filed papers obscuring the file title by positioning the label with the color on the bottom and the file name on the top.
- If you create a new file title, be sure to add it to your File Index.
- Leave at least 3 inches of space in each drawer to allow for additional files.
- Label the outside of file cabinets with their contents.

Step 4: What shall I call it?

- Check the existing File Index to see if an appropriate file already exists for the papers you want to file. If it doesn't, establish a new file by asking: What word would I think of first if I wanted or needed to retrieve this information?
- If you don't have a File Index, create one now. Creating the Index as you go, instead of going back and doing it later, will take less time and will eliminate making a file for "Auto" when you already have one called "Car."

Step 5: How should we evaluate the day's accomplishments?

- Allow thirty minutes at the end of the

day to assess your progress: How much more time do you need to finish the project? When will you do it? What retention questions came up and who can answer them?

- Label all piles and files so that you can easily access the information within them until you finally file everything.

Step 6: How should we maintain our accomplishments?

Make the File Index as user-friendly as possible. While you probably will not have time to complete your revision of the File Index on File Clean-Out Day, you should schedule time to do it as soon as possible to get the greatest return on the time you spent cleaning out. Also:

- Single-space the index, except at the beginning of each alphabetical section, to minimize the number of pages when it is printed out.
- Note the required Retention Guideline beside each index category whenever possible. This will make file clean-out easier next time.
- Use the File Index to keep track of oversized materials, books, or other materials, noting their location.
- Keep a copy of the File Index near the file cabinet or at the desk of everyone who uses the files.
- Update the File Index regularly.

TIP: RECYCLING OPPORTUNITIES

In my early years of organizing File Clean-Out Days, before many organizations were actively involved in recycling, participants would say, "Oh, look at all those trees we're wasting!" when they saw the dumpsters filling up. I responded, "Do you think we're saving them by keeping the paper in the files?" Now, when we bring in recycling containers, participants say, "Oh, look at all the trees we're saving!"

File Clean-Out Day is an excellent opportunity to implement or improve your recycling practices—not just for paper, but for equipment, unneeded supplies, and inventory.

COMPUTER EQUIPMENT

- **Share the Technology** (www .sharetechnology.org) sponsors a national database to help connect computer donors and nonprofit recipients, such as public schools, private schools, nonprofits, and individuals with disabilities. You can search by state for donation requests.
- **Earth 911** (www.1800cleanup.org), a corporate-sponsored Web site, allows you to search by Zip code for local options for recycling of computers and materials.

EXCESS INVENTORY

- **The National Association for the Exchange of Industrial Resources** (NAEIR; 260 McClure St., Galesburg, IL 61401; 800-562-0955; www.naeir.org) is a nonprofit organization that acts as a go-between for its members, such as schools and nonprofit organizations, and companies that wish to make tax-deductible donations of excess inventory.

- What questions have come up from cleaning out your files?
- How much more time do you need to finish this job?
- How could we improve our next File Clean-Out Day?

Members of management should meet with the event coordinator after File Clean-Out Day. They should discuss the evaluation forms and determine what steps to take next and when. These might include:

- Scheduling the next File Clean-Out Day.
- Identifying who will get answers to questions that arise during the process.
- Shifting files from one department to another.
- Ordering new equipment.

■ Updating the file Retention Guidelines.

Compile statistics to document the amount of materials removed from the files. Publicize your results—and your success!

CHAPTER 17

Establish Retention Guidelines

A fter you've completed the inventory of existing files, the next step is to establish user-friendly Retention Guidelines. Often, offices are glutted with paper and computer files because the people who use them aren't given guidelines about what to keep and what to eliminate. Ironically, some organizations do have such guidelines, but they aren't communicated to the people who really need them, or if they are, they aren't provided in an easy-to-use form. For example, one my clients had a retention guidebook that was nearly a hundred pages long, but it was poorly organized, and it contained information that most people didn't need.

As a general rule, Retention Guidelines are most useful when organized individually by each department in the organization, but it's helpful for all departments to know what the others are keeping. For example, in one company I discovered three departments (on the same floor) keeping the same information about prospective meeting sites. This resulted in unnecessary duplication, and took too much space. The three departments also kept the information for several years when, in fact, it wouldn't be wise for them to choose a meeting space based on old information.

Talk With Staff Members

P eople who use files regularly are the best source of information when you're developing Retention Guidelines. Use the records inventory form discussed

TIP: WHAT SHOULD YOU KEEP AND FOR HOW LONG?

Here are some guidelines for keeping some typical business records:

THREE YEARS
- **Monthly financial statements** used for internal purposes

FOUR YEARS
- **Personnel and payroll records,** such as payments and reports to taxing authorities (including those related to federal income tax withholding, FICA contributions, and unemployment taxes) and workers' compensation insurance

SIX YEARS
- **Bank reconciliations,** voided checks, check stubs and check register tapes
- **Canceled, payroll, and dividend checks**
- **Purchase records,** including purchase orders, payment vouchers authorizing payment to vendors, and vendor invoices
- **Sales records,** such as invoices, monthly statements, remittance advisories, shipping papers, bills of lading, and customers' purchase orders
- **Travel and entertainment records,** including account books, diaries, and expense statements

INDEFINITELY
- **Annual financial statements**
- **Books of account,** such as the general ledger and general journal (ledgers refer to the actual books or the magnetic tapes, diskettes, or other media on which the ledgers and journals are stored). These should be kept indefinitely, unless they're regularly posted to the general ledger.
- **Corporate documents,** including certificate of incorporation, corporate charter, constitution and bylaws, deeds and easements, stock, stock transfer and stockholder records, minutes of board of directors' meeting, retirement and pension records, labor contracts, licenses, patents, trademarks and registration applications
- **Documents substantiating fixed-asset additions,** such as the amounts and dates of additions or improvements, detail related to retirements, depreciation policies, and salvage values assigned to assets
- **Income-tax forms,** revenue agents' reports, protests, court briefs and appeals
- **Income-tax payment checks**

previously (see the box on page 160) as a starting point for discussion. Try to determine whether people are actually using the information that is kept and have them anticipate how long they may continue to use it. Employees may not know the answers to either question, which is exactly the reason for going through this process.

Talk With Your Advisers

To further develop your Retention Guidelines, collect all the information you can from your accountant and general counsel about what information is legally necessary to keep in your company (and see the box at left for suggestions). If your organization belongs to an industry-related association, it might be able to provide you with additional Retention Guidelines.

The Originator's Rule: The Universal Retention Guideline

It's unnecessary and undesirable to keep duplicate information. One way to avoid this is to be sure that everyone in your office understands and implements, wherever applicable, the Originator's Rule: Whoever originates a piece of paper is responsible for its retention. This relieves everyone else from keeping unnecessary back-up copies.

Document Your Record-Keeping Plan

Once you've collected all the available information about records retention from internal and external sources, it's time to put the information in some sort of user-friendly form for each department by adding the information to your File Index.

If your company becomes involved in litigation or an audit, you'll be in a much better position to protect yourself if you produce evidence of your records-retention program. Having a formal records-retention program creates consistency and indicates an honest attempt to retain important information. For example, if you're audited and you have only some records, at best you will look sloppy, and at worst, you will give the impression that you're trying to hide something.

It's a good idea to set up and maintain a computer

Whoever originates a piece of paper is responsible for its retention.

RESOURCE: FOR MORE INFORMATION

If you need more information about Retention Guidelines for your organization, check out these resources:

- **ARMA International** (The Association for Information Management Professionals, 13725 W. 109th St., Lenexa, KS 66215; 800-422-2762; www.arma.org)
- *Information and Records Management: Document Based Information Systems,* by Mary Robek, Gerald F. Brown, and David O. Stephens ($67; Glencoe McGraw Hill)
- *Recordkeeping Requirements,* by Donald S. Skupsky ($45 plus shipping and handling; Information Requirements Clearinghouse, 5600 South Quebec St., Suite 250-C, Englewood, CO 80111; 303-721-7500; www.irch .com). Because this item was last published in 1994, some of the information may be dated; however, it still offers many good ideas.

database of the company's records, including the location of all records and how long they must be kept. This will give you the flexibility to sort the information into various types of lists as needed.

CHAPTER 18

Create a New (or Renewed) Filing System

Okay, now you've eliminated unnecessary information in your office or organization. The next step is to organize what you do need to keep. In many offices, the filing systems have more or less evolved without any real planning.

As we discussed earlier, it's essential to designate one person who will be responsible for making sure that the filing system is effective. He or she might be called the file-systems manager, information-resources manager, or records-resource manager. This person should work with each department to identify its resources and assist in the design and implementation of its filing system. You could choose one person to fill this role, or a "task force," depending on the needs of the department or organization. Is the organization or department willing to live by one person's decision? If not, then a task force is in order.

The easiest way to analyze your file system is by looking at the current File Index, which you created or updated on File Clean-Out Day. If you tried instead to take inventory of the drawers themselves, by the time you got to the end of the second drawer, you wouldn't remember what was in the first drawer—much less many offices full of file drawers. (If you're using *Taming the Paper Tiger* software, use the File Retention Worksheet.)

Can you tell by looking at the index how to quickly file or find any document in your department? If your system is in relatively good shape, you and other staff members may need only to rearrange a few files. But, if your organization is like most that I've seen, a major overhaul may be in order. In that case, the best approach might be to start over.

If You Need to Start Over

Here are some suggestions for creating a workable and efficient filing system:

First, design your system on paper, by creating or revising the department File Index. Human nature is such that we buy in to a system when we have the opportunity to participate in its design, so it will be helpful to at least talk with employees to identify what they like and don't like about the existing system.

One of the major contributors to confusing filing systems is having too many categories. Put information in its largest general categories first. These might include: Administration, Clients, Financial, and Resources. I create a new category when that subject takes up more than one-half of a file drawer. For example, if all the information you have about travel takes only a few files, they would be filed under "T" in Administration. However, I keep extensive information about travel, so I've created a Travel category in a separate drawer.

After you've identified the major categories, assign a number to each category. For example, Accounting In-

TIP: SIX STEPS TO ORGANIZING THE ORGANIZATION

1. Assign someone to be responsible for organizing the information.
2. Identify the information that is essential to your organization and establish Retention Guidelines.
3. Conduct a File Clean-Out Day (see Chapter 16), at least annually.
4. Complete an inventory of the existing files and create a user-friendly index of your files.
5. Complete an inventory and create an index of other types of information.
6. Use your inventory of files and other types of information to create an Information Resource Directory and update it annually.

formation could be assigned 1; Administrative files could be assigned 2, and so on. Then go through your index of all the existing files, deleting or adding new files when appropriate, and beside each file title, mark the number (1, 2, and so on) of the major category in which that file belongs. Now redo the index by putting all the 1's together, all the 2's together, and so on, and alphabetize the files within their categories.

Create your new File Index by reorganizing all like file titles in the most appropriate way. In an alphabetical filing system, use basic alphabetizing rules:

- **Alphabetize** last names first; for example, Ann Adamson would be filed as: Adamson, Ann.
- **Consider prefixes** as part of a name; for example, St. John, Oliver would be indexed under S.
- **Arrange hyphenated names** as written; for example, First-Hartling, Laura would be indexed under F.
- **Arrange company names** as written; for example, Manhattan School of Music would be indexed under M.
- **At the beginning of a name,** disregard "The"; for example, The Center for Advanced Studies would be indexed under C as: Center for Advanced Studies, (The).
- **Political divisions** are indexed with major name first; for example, U.S. Department of Agriculture is indexed as: United States Government, Agriculture (Dept. Of).

Make the physical files match the system and File Index that you created. Pull together all the files assigned 1, all files assigned 2, and so on.

Separate out old records, and from them, those that are vital. Put the vital records in a safe storage place, preferably off-site, and put the old records someplace other than prime office space. To calculate the difference in cost between storing your records on site versus off site, try the calculator provided at www.recordstorage.com/calculator.htm. If you choose an off-site facility to store inactive records, make sure it's clean, climate-controlled, secure, and insulated. The

TIP: THE MATTER OF FORMS

According to a study by International Data Corporation, 83% of all business documents consists of forms. Businesses in the U.S. annually spend about $1 billion to design and print forms and another $25 billion to $35 billion to store and retrieve them, and, over the entire life cycle of those documents, a whopping $65 billion to $85 billion to maintain, update, and distribute them.

Whenever I organize an office, one of the first steps I take is to request from all employees a copy of every form they use or have on hand. I frequently get several versions of the same form, as well as forms that no one is using. Here are some steps that can improve that situation:

- **Identify which paper forms** you can replace with electronic ones.
- **Gather the remaining paper forms** in a central location. Employees can still keep copies of frequently used forms at their desks if they like.
- **If there are only a few forms,** file them in the administrative files under "F."

- **If there are many forms,** assign one file drawer and label it "Forms." File the forms alphabetically by their official names and create an index of forms accordingly that will be located in the front of the drawer.
- **If you don't have a computer original** of a form and you create new forms by photocopying, then keep one copy of each form in a plastic page protector. Label that version "File Copy—Do Not Remove," which will minimize the possibility of someone taking the last copy.
- **When applicable,** make a note of where new forms can be obtained.
- **If forms are entirely computerized,** create a computer directory called "Forms" and file all forms there. Make sure that anyone who will need access to the files has the appropriate permissions to use them.
- **If your organization** has some forms in hard copy and some in the computer, use the index of forms to indicate both types and their location.

storage company should be bonded and insured against fire and flood.

Label boxes or files clearly, indicating their contents and destruction dates. Failure to select a date for destruction—or at least a review—will mean unnecessary storage expense and a massive cleanup project in the future. Keep a record of stored files in an easily accessible place (for example, in your administrative files under "Records Storage, Off-Site") so that it can be referred to and updated.

A Centrally Understood Filing System

Not so long ago, most organizations had a central filing system controlled by one person. "Central Files" referred to a specific location, such as a file room or a large bank of files, where everyone filed information that was of use to the department or the organization. If you wanted a piece of paper, you had to ask "Mabel." When you were finished, you returned the paper to Mabel, confident that she would refile it and find it again as needed. Centralized files, with information kept in one place, increased administrative control over the filing system, minimized misfiled and lost documents, and made routine review and destruction less complicated.

Then many businesses chose to reduce office space and personnel, eliminating space for a central file room and money for Mabel. Soon filing cabinets were tucked in corners around the office, and employees throughout the company began filling them with paper. Before long, those cabinets were a dumping ground for papers that no one really cared about, while individual offices filled up with paper because their occupants were afraid to use what passed for the central files. Does this sound familiar?

Today, even if Mabel were still around, space constraints would make it difficult to maintain a central location for files. However, the concept of central filing is still valuable and possible by developing a master plan of the filing system, which clearly accounts for and identifies file cabinets in various locations. I often refer to this strategy as a "Centrally Understood Filing System." This simply means that the files, as well as other kinds of resources, are physically located in the most logical place for the people who use them, but are also available for anyone else who needs them. The key to a centrally understood file system is the Information Resource Directory.

> The concept of central filing is still valuable and possible by developing a master plan of the filing system.

> After you've organized your hard copy and computer files, it's time to look at the other sources of information in your office that need to be organized.

Create Your Information Resource Directory

Just as organizations identify their valuable human resources with an organization chart and their financial resources with a budget, they should be able to easily identify the valuable and essential information found in their filing systems and computers, bookshelves and desks. I call the tool designed for this purpose an Information Resource Directory. It's similar to your File Index, except that it inventories all information resources, whatever their location.

After you've organized your hard copy and computer files, it's time to look at the other sources of information in your office that need to be organized. Begin by putting like items together—in this case, by type of media: Computer diskettes, tapes or CDs, microfilm, card files, books, pamphlets, notebooks, audiotapes and videotapes, and so on.

Within each type of media, group items by subject, such as advertising or management. You may choose to alphabetize them within the subject category, but in my experience, it's not worth the time. However, you can use a colored dot on the binding (or case) to indicate the subject. For example, all management books could have red dots, while all marketing books could have yellow dots. This identification will encourage people to return items to the proper location.

Apply the same organizing principles to these items as you did to the traditional files:

- **Eliminate unnecessary items** by discarding, recycling, returning, or merging. For example, if several employees receive the same publications, set up a central library and eliminate the duplicate subscriptions (see the box at right). Or, if everyone maintains a personal file of interoffice memos, set up a central file (or binder) where they are arranged by subject, date, or author.
- **Determine the most appropriate location** for everything, whether the storage room, mail room, bookshelves in X's office or cupboard in Y's office, and so on.

TIP: SAVINGS ON SUBSCRIPTIONS

One of my clients had an entire room full of newsletters, magazines, audiotapes, and video-tapes. We inventoried the contents of the room, noting just the names of the publications, not the specific issues on hand. We circulated the resulting list and asked employees to check off those they used. More than 80% of the publications were not checked! Consider the cost of purchasing those publications, organizing them, and then storing them. This client saved plenty of money just by eliminating the excess.

- **Identify the best container for the items,** such as magazine-type containers, closed boxes, open baskets, ringed binders, and so on.
- **Label all locations** and containers clearly.

Finally, make a list of all resources categorized by location and place in a loose-leaf notebook or a computer file. These categories might include: hard-copy files, computer files (you could add a copy of your computer File Index), bookshelves, storage cabinets, and even individual desks, if other members of the organization might need the information located there.

This notebook should be easily available to everyone who uses the information resources in your office. If you prepare your Information Resource Directory in a computer file, you will need to make certain that everyone who needs to can access it at will, although they may have read-only privileges; you don't want just anyone editing the directory.

Be sure to update the Information Resource Directory at least once a year when you complete your annual File Clean-Out Day.

Imagine how pleased new employees would be to receive the directory. A graduate student told me that he spent the first three weeks of an internship looking for information he needed to complete the project he had been hired to do. Obviously, this was a waste of his

RESOURCE: SOME TOOLS

These tools will facilitate creating your Information Resource Directory:

- **www.thepapertiger.com.** This software can be used to index paper files, binders, electronic media, photography, and other physical resources so that they can be easily shared.
- **www.irch.com.** This records-retention software implements the Skupsky Retention Method, described in the book by Donald Skupsky listed on page 174.
- **www.assetverification.com.** This product uses voice-activated software and digital imaging to inventory property, the results of which are recorded on a CD-ROM.

time, certainly not cost-effective, and could have been avoided if the organization had had an Information Resource Directory.

On the Road to Success

In every organizing process, things might get worse before they get better. This is natural and unavoidable.

It would be wonderful if we could stop the telephones, the mail, and the interruptions for a few days—or weeks—while we get organized, but in the real world that's not possible. This means that you may have to organize in stages.

As you proceed, continually ask yourself: Does this work? Do I like it? If your organizing will affect the people around you, ask: Does it work for others? If you get a negative answer to any of those questions, keep trying—and don't be afraid to ask for help if you need it.

Getting organized is not glamorous, but it's a critical component of a healthy, productive office. My experience is that the more organized people or organizations become, the more willing they are to toss stuff out. We tend to think that piles of disorganized information contain information that would be very useful if we could

RESOURCES: BARBARA HEMPHILL

If you have questions about the ideas that I've presented in this book, or you would like information about speaking or consulting services or other organizing products, please feel free to contact: The Hemphill Productivity Institute (1464 Garner Station Blvd., #330, Raleigh, NC 27603; 919-773-0722, phone; 919-773-0383, fax; Barbara@productiveEnvironment.com; www.productiveEnvironment.com).

but find it. It's only after we get the information organized that we can measure whether we will really use it.

Frequently, clients ask me, "How long is this project going to take?" and often my answer is: "I don't know, but I do know that the longer you wait to get organized, the longer the process will take and the more difficult it will be. So the sooner you begin, the better. I know that you will reap rewards for your effort!"

Index

F

FAT system
backlogs and, 28–30
decisions to make, 19
e-mail and, 86–89
fear of throwing things out, 20
"In" boxes and, 26–28
Information Management Flowchart, 19, 22, 30–31
logic-based disposal, 20–21, 23
retention guidelines, 23, 25–26
voice mail and, 89
before you begin, 30
Fax machines, 120, 124
File Clean-Out Day
archiving and, 165
computers and, 99–100, 162
coordinator for, 162–163, 168–169
establishing, 112, 144
file indexes and, 175
Information Resource Directory and, 181
locating missing documents, 162
meeting after, 168–169
organizing, 161–169
recycling tips, 168
selecting the day, 161
steps to follow, 166–167
"what to do if" tipsheet, 164
File folders, 37–40
File indexes
for computer filing systems, 98
creating a new system and, 175–177, 180–181
description, 49
example, 50–51

"File Clean-Out Day" and, 175
importance of, 112
Information Resource Directories and, 180
starting, 49
taking to conventions, 139
tips, 50–52
updating, 50, 52, 112, 175
Files, categories for action, 77–83, 131
Filing cabinets
calendars as, 60
computer filing systems compared with, 92–93
for home offices, 118–119
purchasing pointers, 36
Filing systems. *See also* Computer filing systems
Action files, 37
analyzing, 175–176
assigning responsibilities for, 111–112, 157–159, 175
breakdown in, 48–49
calendars and, 60
card files, 44, 54, 57
categories, 46–47, 176–177
central filing concept, 179
cleaning out, 61, 111
colored files and labels, 41–42
creating a new system, 175–183
cross-referencing, 47
designing, 45–52
destruction dates for files, 178
FAT system, 19–31
"File Clean-Out Day," 99–100, 112, 144, 161–169
file folders, 37–40
filing according to use, 46

forms and, 178
indexes for, 48–52, 98, 112, 139, 175–177, 180–181
key words, 43–44
labeling files, 40–41, 165, 178
maintaining, 111–114
old records, 177–178
open-shelf, 36–37, 39–40
organizations and, 152–153
oversized items, 39
portable filing boxes, 38
for projects or events, 84–85
"*See also*" references, 47
simplicity and, 45–46
starting over versus fixing the system, 47–48
stumbling blocks to success, 112–114
tips, 42–44
tools for, 36–40
updating, 50, 52
vital records, 177–178
Financial management programs, 107–108
First Things First, 69, 72
"Follow-me" service for telephones, 121–122
Forms, 178

G

Groupware, 105–106

H

Home offices
basic equipment for, 122–125
challenges to, 119
comfort in, 117–118
computers for, 122–124
copy machines, 124–125
creating a suitable workspace, 117–122